Merci, de tout cœur,
pour votre charmant
accueil, et notre délicieux
séjour parmi vous
toute notre affection
Louis Jacqui

MR. & Mme L.J. CARTIER

Monsieur et Madame P. Cartier
15 East 96th Street
New York City.

NEW YORK N.Y.
MAR 26
1927

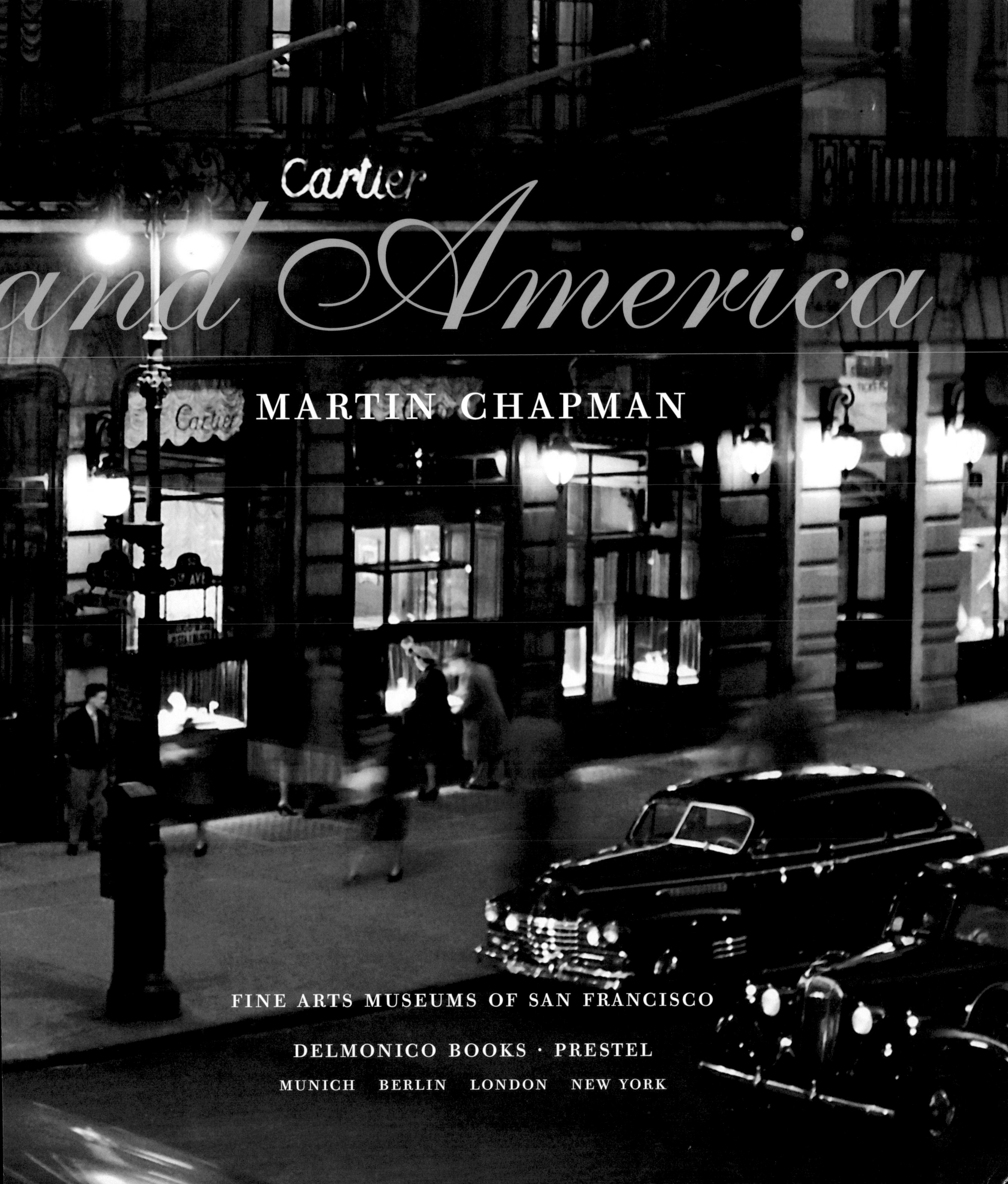

Cartier

and America

MARTIN CHAPMAN

FINE ARTS MUSEUMS OF SAN FRANCISCO

DELMONICO BOOKS · PRESTEL

MUNICH   BERLIN   LONDON   NEW YORK

For Judy Rudoe

Published in 2009 by the Fine Arts Museums of San Francisco and DelMonico Books,
an imprint of Prestel Publishing, on the occasion of the exhibition *Cartier and America*, curated by Martin Chapman.

Legion of Honor
December 19, 2009–April 18, 2010

Cartier and America is organized by the Fine Arts Museums of San Francisco in partnership with Cartier.

MAJOR PATRON

Lonna Wais

SPONSORS

Mr. and Mrs. Adolphus Andrews, Jr.

Dr. Alan R. Malouf

Official Airline

Copyright © 2009 by the Fine Arts Museums of San Francisco.
Layout and design © Prestel Verlag, Munich • Berlin • London • New York. All rights reserved. No part of this book may be reproduced or transmitted in any form or by any means, electronic or mechanical, including photocopy, recording, or any other information storage and retrieval system, or otherwise without written permission from the publisher.

Fine Arts Museums of San Francisco
Golden Gate Park
50 Hagiwara Tea Garden Drive
San Francisco, CA 94118-4502

Director of Publications: Ann Heath Karlstrom
Editor in Chief: Karen A. Levine

Prestel, a member of Verlagsgruppe Random House GmbH

Prestel Verlag
Königinstrasse 9
80539 Munich
Germany
Tel: 49 89 24 29 08 300
Fax: 49 89 24 29 08 335
www.prestel.de

Prestel Publishing Ltd.
4 Bloomsbury Place
London WC1A 2QA
United Kingdom
Tel: 44 20 7323 5004
Fax: 44 20 7636 8004

Prestel Publishing
900 Broadway. Suite 603
New York, NY 10003
Tel: 212 995 2720
Fax: 212 995 2733
E-mail: sales@prestel-usa.com
www.prestel.com

Library of Congress Control Number: 2009937194
ISBN: 978-3-7913-5015-8

Frontispiece: *Visiting card with envelope*, Cartier New York, ca. 1927
A gold thank-you card sent by Louis and Jacqueline Cartier of Paris to Pierre and Elma Cartier for entertaining them in New York in 1927. [cat. 122]

Title page: View of Cartier's store at the corner of Fifth Avenue and 52nd Street, New York, 1947

References to cat. numbers in text and captions correspond with the catalogue of the exhibition (pp. 158–176), where complete information about each artwork appears.

Edited by Karen A. Levine
Designed and typeset by Katy Homans
Preface translated from the French by Alison Anderson
Printed in Singapore by CS Graphics Pte Ltd

PHOTOGRAPHY CREDITS

Unless otherwise indicated below, each illustration is reproduced by permission of the owner of the work identified in the catalogue of the exhibition (pp. 158–176) and/or in the image caption.

Jacket: front: Edward Owen for Hillwood Estate, Museum & Gardens; back: Photofest
Frontispiece (p. 1): Nick Welsh, Cartier Collection, © Cartier
Title page (pp. 2–3): Alfred Eisenstaedt / Time & Life Pictures / Getty Images

Plates: 1, 7, 15–17, 20, 23, 27, 30, 33, 35, 57, 60–61, 97, 154–156: Cartier Archives, © Cartier; 2, 11, 13–14, 99: © Bettmann/Corbis; 3: © Jack Nisberg / Roger-Viollet; 4–5, 8, 18–19, 21–22, 36–42, 44–45, 47–56, 63–84, 86–96, 100–103, 105–113, 115–120, 122–123, 126–127, 134–135, 137–140, 150–153, 157–159, 161–162, 164: Nick Welsh, Cartier Collection, © Cartier; 6: Martin Chapman; 9: Cecil Beaton, © Condé Nast Publications; 10: Chip Clark, © Smithsonian Institution / Corbis; 12: Christian Creutz, © Cartier; 24: © Ministère de la culture—Médiathèque du Patrimoine / François Kollar / dist. RMN; 25–26, 46, 85, 98, 114, 121: Edward Owen for Hillwood Estate, Museum & Gardens; 28, 59: courtesy the Cecil Beaton Studio Archive at Sotheby's; 29: Eve Johnson / Archive Films / Getty Images; 31: Ian Reeves for the Fine Arts Museums of San Francisco; 32: Royal Collection © 2009 Her Majesty Queen Elizabeth II; 34 43, 136: Joe McDonald for the Fine Arts Museums of San Francisco; 58: © E. O. Hoppé / Corbis; 62, 163: Doug Rosa for Siegelson, New York; 104, 124: courtesy Sotheby's; 125: Louis Tirilly, © Cartier; 128: © 2009 SquareMoose; 130: G. Lukomski, © Palais Princier de Monaco; 131: Jon Brenneis / Time & Life Pictures / Getty Images; 132: © GIA & Tino Hammid; 133: Lord Snowdon, courtesy Creative Talent Ltd; 141–143: John Bigelow Taylor; 144–149: © Palais Princier de Monaco

Catalogue: 1–23, 25–32, 35–51, 53–62, 65–70, 72–111, 113–127, 129–130, 132–140, 142–150, 152–169, 171–177, 179–185, 187–203, 205, 207–211, 213–217, 219–227, 230, 235–238, 241–243, 245, 250, 252–253, 255–256, 258, 261–269, 271–276: Nick Welsh, Cartier Collection, © Cartier; 24, 259: Joe McDonald for the Fine Arts Museums of San Francisco; 34, 71, 141, 178, 186, 228–229: Edward Owen for Hillwood Estate, Museum & Gardens; 52: Christian Creutz, © Cartier; 63, 112, 131, 170: Doug Rosa for Siegelson, New York; 128, 206, 270, 277: © GIA & Tino Hammid; 151: © 2009 SquareMoose; 204: Louis Tirilly, © Cartier; 231–233: John Bigelow Taylor; 234, 240, 278: courtesy Sotheby's; 239, 244, 246–249, 251, 254 260: © Palais Princier de Monaco; 279: Ian Reeves for the Fine Arts Museums of San Francisco

Contents

Foreword

The Fine Arts Museums of San Francisco are proud to present *Cartier and America*, marking the hundredth anniversary of that firm in the United States. This exhibition at the Legion of Honor demonstrates the enduring connections between France and the United States through a wonderful array of Cartier jewelry, clocks, and works of art that were either supplied to Americans or made here between 1902 and 2007.

Several of the founding donors to the Legion of Honor were significant Cartier clients. As a result of her fund-raising efforts for France and other Allied countries during World War I, Alma de Bretteville Spreckels formed a wide network of friends who donated to her new museum, conceived as a memorial to Californian veterans. One of the first major gifts came in 1922 from Grand Duchess Kyrill of Russia. Between 1911 and 1913 she acquired several pieces of jewelry from Cartier's store in Paris, including a diamond bandeau, a pearl-and-diamond pendant, and a chain of sapphires and diamonds. Spreckels's connection to the grand duchess came through her sister, Queen Marie of Romania, who was also one of Cartier's clients. The English-born sisters were known for their elegantly royal, if somewhat eccentric, style of dress, often enhanced with Cartier jewelry. Having lost her jewels during World War I, Queen Marie asked Cartier Paris to supply her with new pieces around 1920. These included a pearl-and-diamond bandeau that she wore "Byzantine-style," complemented by a long diamond chain with a massive sapphire pendant. Another significant Cartier client connected to the early years of the Legion was Arabella Huntington, whose collection of eighteenth-century French art was donated to the museum by her son, Archer Huntington. Reputedly the richest woman in America in 1900, she was an avid wearer of pearls purchased from Cartier Paris between 1902 and 1910. Most famous was a strand of black pearls set in diamonds, known as the Duchess of Hamilton pearls. As related in this catalogue, several of Cartier's customers had connections with San Francisco and the Bay Area, making it fitting that we hold *Cartier and America* here at the Fine Arts Museums.

I begin my acknowledgments by thanking museum patron Lonna Wais, who provided us with the entrée to Cartier. In addition, I thank curator Martin Chapman for his guidance of this exhibition and catalogue. He has devoted himself tirelessly to the excellence of the project. Karen Levine, editor in chief, edited with remarkable precision and produced this publication in record time. I also thank Krista Brugnara, Bill White, Therese Chen, and Melissa Buron. We are all tremendously appreciative of Cartier's staff in Paris, London, Geneva, and New York, who have done so much to enable this venture. Pierre Rainero and Vivian Thatos deserve thanks for initiating the project. In New York, Gregory Bishop and Violette Petit provided us with much-needed expertise and access to the

6

1. Queen Marie of Romania in 1921 wearing jewels supplied by Cartier Paris. The pendant to the diamond sautoir was the largest cut sapphire in the world (478 carats).

remarkable archives. In Paris, Renée Frank, Gaëlle Naegellen, and Hélène Ribatet Godard attended to the many details of the exhibition, while Michel Aliaga and Françoise Benoist helped with the client history. Archivist Betty Jais provided a steady stream of information that has greatly enhanced this catalogue. In London, archivist Charlotte Batchelor helped with many questions concerning expatriate Americans. In Geneva, Pascale Lepeu, curator of the Cartier Collection, graciously assisted with the choice of objects. Additional thanks go to Celine Daudin-Bollinger, Monique Gay, and Nadia Cretignier.

A number of other individuals have been crucial to this catalogue and exhibition. Thanks are due particularly to Judy Rudoe, Ralph Esmerian, Liana Paredes, Christopher Forbes, Harry Fane of Obsidian, London, Lady Alexander of Weedon, Suzanne Tennenbaum, Alice Dugdale, Hervé Irien, Alan Hart, Douglas Weimer, Philip Hewat Jaboor, Yassi and Craig Castilla, Lisa Hubbard, Shelley Bennett, Mary DelMonico, and Katy Homans.

I cannot conclude without expressing deepest gratitude to our lenders, whose generosity has given rise to the richness and variety of this presentation. The Cartier Collection, Geneva, is the source of most of the pieces on display. Significant works are also coming to us from Hillwood Estate, Museum & Gardens; Neil Lane, Los Angeles; the Lindemann Collection; HSH Prince Albert II and the Palais Princier de Monaco; Siegelson, New York; Dame Elizabeth Taylor; Diane B. Wilsey; and several private collectors. The presentation is made possible through the indispensable support of Lonna Wais, with additional sponsorship from BNP Paribas, Mr. and Mrs. Adolphus Andrews, Jr., Dr. Alan R. Malouf, Emirates, and Campton Place.

JOHN E. BUCHANAN, JR.
Director of Museums   Fine Arts Museums of San Francisco

Preface

In 1909 Pierre Cartier, the second of three brothers, moved into 712 Fifth Avenue in New York. He very soon acquired a private mansion on the corner of Fifth Avenue and 52nd Street that had been built for Morton F. Plant, in exchange for a magnificent natural pearl necklace that the businessman's wife had set her heart on. Today this building remains Cartier's headquarters in the United States. The story behind that spectacular transaction continues to reflect the relationship between Cartier and America, a relationship that is both exalted and intimate. Members of the American meritocracy became leading clients, thus establishing privileged ties. Among them were the pioneers of the New World: financiers, adventurers, politicians; great artists, Hollywood and Broadway stars; and, of course, patrons of the arts in a country of boundless creativity and energy.

In 1997 the Metropolitan Museum of Art, New York, mounted a memorable exhibition in celebration of Cartier's 150th anniversary. In 2001 the mayor of New York baptized the intersection of Fifth Avenue and 52nd Street *Place de Cartier*, officially acknowledging Cartier's significant role in the history of the city and country.

Cartier's esteemed clientele are also to be found on the West Coast. Hollywood became the epicenter of a love story between Cartier and the reigning sovereigns of the cinema, who have worn Cartier both in real life and on-screen: Rudolf Valentino, Gloria Swanson, Marlene Dietrich, Marilyn Monroe, Elizabeth Taylor . . .

In 2009 Cartier commemorates a century of French-American friendship. The exhibition organized by the Fine Arts Museums of San Francisco closes a year of celebrations with an important retrospective devoted to the ties between Cartier and America. It is hard to imagine a more appropriate venue to host the presentation than the California Palace of the Legion of Honor, a three-quarter-scale version of the *hôtel particulier* now known as the Palais de la Légion d'Honneur, located on the banks of the Seine in Paris. Founded by the Francophile Alma de Bretteville Spreckels in 1915, this prestigious establishment has maintained a tradition of artistic and cultural exchange with France. At the entrance to the museum Rodin's *Thinker* keeps watch, and the motto inscribed on the frieze is a reminder of French tradition: "Honneur et Patrie."

At Cartier, therefore, we are very proud to share our long history with the museums and visitors of San Francisco. Through exchanges between our two continents, from one ocean to another, Cartier revives the memory of those great American clients who have enriched its destiny.

I would like to thank, in particular, Diane Wilsey, president of the Board of Trustees, and John E. Buchanan, Jr., director of the Fine Arts Museums, for their enthusiastic

2. Pierre Cartier
playing golf in
Miami, ca. 1930

involvement in this project; Martin Chapman, the erudite and passionate curator of the exhibition; and the entire staff of the Museums for their professionalism. I would also like to express my gratitude to the institutions, private collectors, and major clients who have lent essential works, without which this exhibition would not have been complete, and with whom we are writing a new page in Cartier's history.

BERNARD FORNAS
President and CEO Cartier

Cartier for Americans

"Let me introduce you to the man who killed Rasputin," Lady Emerald Cunard once announced to her guests at lunch. Not surprisingly, the Grand Duke Dmitri Pavlovich—who had indeed had a hand in dispatching the old menace—turned on his heel and left.[1]

Lady Cunard (1872–1948), who was born Maud Burke in San Francisco, was the notoriously outspoken American leader of London high society between the wars. Married to the heir of the Cunard steamship fortune, she was part of the cosmopolitan circle surrounding the Prince of Wales and his American friend, Wallis Simpson. In the mid-1930s nearly all of the members of this circle were avid customers of Cartier's London branch, and among them Lady Cunard was the jeweler's most devoted patron. Her client account reveals that she went into the shop with astonishing frequency between 1928 and 1940. In 1929 alone there were forty-three orders to her account, including four grand diamond-set necklaces, two diamond bracelets, and a diamond-and-emerald brooch. She even had the fabric replaced on an evening bag and a vanity case converted into a cigarette case. The firm's trade in fashionable jewelry, its wide range of luxury accessories, and its repair and alteration services meant that for Lady Cunard there were many reasons to visit Cartier's shop at 145 New Bond Street.[2]

Americans have always been important customers for Cartier. Even before the Parisian jeweler opened its business on rue de la Paix in 1899, Americans such as J. P. Morgan were patrons of Cartier's previous store on the boulevard des Italiens.[3] However, when Cartier moved to the more fashionable rue de la Paix, Americans—fueled by their recently acquired industrial riches—became an increasingly significant clientele. By 1900, when the hugely successful Exposition Universelle drew fifty million visitors, Paris was confirmed as the luxury center of the world, attracting a whole new generation of customers. Cartier was one of the destinations for Americans visiting Paris because it had a reputation for making the finest jewelry for the ruling elites. In the early years of the century, it was *de rigueur* for American women to dress at Worth on rue de la Paix and to complement their attire with jewelry from Cartier, just next door. The novelist Elinor Glyn wrote

3. Grace Kelly and Prince Rainier III of Monaco shopping at Cartier Paris before their wedding, ca. 1955

in 1908 that she admired Americans who "crossed the Atlantic twice a year to have their dresses fitted and whose jewels were perfect."[4] Cartier's jewelry was the supreme example of this essential measure of refinement and precision, and its success during those years was the result of important innovations in the business.

With the move of the store to rue de la Paix, Alfred Cartier (1841–1925) also shifted his business model, repositioning the firm as a designer and manufacturer of jewelry rather than a retailer of luxury goods. He transformed the firm in three significant ways in order to suit an expanding market for expensive and precious items: by taking closer control over manufacturing, by adopting a particular program for design, and by establishing new branches abroad. He wanted to ensure that Cartier would become renowned worldwide for its exceptional craftsmanship, refined designs, and use of high-quality gemstones—a reputation that it did indeed achieve in the following decades.

With regard to manufacturing, although the firm would continue the practice of commissioning work from some of the many small specialist workshops in Paris, Cartier now prided itself on providing its own designs and having jewelry made in its own designated workshops, thus keeping stricter control over quality. The resulting jewelry was the key to Cartier's success. During the first decade of the century, white diamond jewelry was the fashion for wearing with the sumptuous evening dresses of the Belle Epoque. The new wealth of diamonds that had been mined in South Africa since the 1870s was the perfect match for the newly rich of industry and commerce; indeed, diamonds eclipsed all other gemstones in the years leading up to World War I. Only occasionally were diamonds combined with other gems, such as pearls.

Having espoused the courtly taste for white diamonds, Cartier then implemented the relatively new idea of setting the stones in platinum. Instead of the silver used hitherto, Cartier employed platinum to produce mountings that did not tarnish and gave a more refined overall effect. Overcoming the inherent difficulties of the metal, such as its high melting point, Cartier exploited the means whereby platinum, which had been known but overlooked for well over century, could be worked into the most delicate settings for jewelry. Apart from anything else, it meant that a plentiful supply of diamonds could be compressed into a setting without making the piece too heavy, as would have happened with silver or gold. What Cartier developed in platinum technology in 1900 stood the firm in good stead for the next thirty-five years.[5]

Recognizing the importance of his client base, Cartier completely avoided the contemporary Art Nouveau aesthetic, concentrating instead on what he knew the ruling classes of 1900 wanted: the more conservative Louis XVI style. Derived from the neoclassicism of the late eighteenth century, the Louis XVI revival had enjoyed some popularity since the mid-nineteenth century, most famously in the spectacular diamond jewelry made for the Empress Eugénie in the 1850s and 1860s. The swags and garlands found in pattern books of the late eighteenth century were translated into Cartier's jewelry of around 1900. Often described as Garland style for its frequent use of that type of ornament, the design is inspired by more than that one motif. It includes the full panoply of decoration of the late eighteenth century, ranging from bows and tassels to the vases and medallions that were found in jewelry design albums and architectural design books. Cartier's essentially pretty and feminine application of this style to jewelry suited the conservative taste of the rich and integrated successfully with the prevailing fashions, especially with Worth's elaborately constructed dresses. This close relationship to couture was to remain an important aspect of Cartier's designs in succeeding decades.[6]

The third innovation that made Cartier so successful was the expansion of the business abroad. In 1900, observing that his richest customers came from London, New York, and Saint Petersburg, Cartier investigated opening boutiques in those three cities. In the end he decided not to establish permanent premises in Saint Petersburg, restricting his presence there to visits twice a year, but he proceeded to open shops in London in 1902 and in New York in 1909. Business there was so good that Cartier expanded out of the original premises within a few years, with the London branch moving to 145 New Bond Street and the New York branch to 653 Fifth Avenue—the addresses where they remain today.

Cartier cemented the success of his strategy by deploying his three sons to run the three businesses. Louis (1875–1942), the aesthete and collector, stayed in Paris, which remained the heart of Cartier production. Jacques (1884–1942) moved to London, from which location he also dealt with the lucrative Indian trade.[7] And most significantly for this essay, Pierre (1878–1965, pl. 2), who had originally worked in London, moved to New York to oversee the branch that opened there in 1909. Pierre Cartier's business acumen was essential for dealing with American millionaires; in 1908 he had achieved greater credibility by marrying Elma Rumsey, the daughter of a well-to-do American industrialist from Saint Louis.

CARTIER IN THE GILDED AGE

In the early years of the twentieth century, Cartier actively sought the patronage of the courts of Europe, which were undergoing a brilliant final era. The 1902 coronation of Edward VII (1841–1910) in London, for example, brought Cartier a large number of commissions for tiaras and other grand jewelry—one of the reasons the firm opened a branch in that city. Although Alfred Cartier's Parisian business was directed more toward the middle classes during the second half of the nineteenth century, he had briefly opened a London business that supplied the English royal family with luxury goods in the early 1870s, while the chaos of the Commune was raging in Paris. This experience brought him the business of Edward VII, who, unlike his stolid mother, Queen Victoria, was a great

4. *Tiara*

CARTIER PARIS, 1905

Sold to Mrs. Richard Townsend of Washington, D.C., this tiara shows that Americans wore grand head ornaments in the years leading up to World War I. It is designed in Cartier's signature Louis XVI style.
[cat. 9]

Francophile and an enjoyer of luxury and the good life. He became an important client of the firm as soon as he became king, with the 1901 commission of an Indian-style necklace for Queen Alexandra, and it is he who is said to have dubbed Cartier "King of jewellers and jeweller of kings." He gave Cartier its first royal warrant, naming it an official supplier in 1904. Between that date and 1939 Cartier received fifteen of these royal warrants from various courts, ranging from Edward VII to King Zog of Albania. Apart from the business the warrants brought, Cartier capitalized on them as tools for promotion; the arms of its royal patrons were emblazoned on the fronts of its stores and on its stationery.

Alfred Cartier, recognizing that the patronage of the royal courts would prompt the aspiring new rich of industry and commerce to follow in their wake, supplied his American clients with equally splendid, if not more so, arrays of jewelry. Mary Scott Townsend of Washington, D.C., heir to the fortune of the coal and railroad magnate William Lawrence Scott of Pennsylvania, acquired a suite of diamond jewelry from Cartier

5. *Rose-and-lily corsage ornament*
CARTIER PARIS, 1906

Mrs. Richard Townsend complemented her grand tiara with this substantial breast ornament of entwined roses and lilies. [cat. 14]

Paris in 1905–1906, perhaps in preparation for her daughter Mathilde's debut in 1907.[8] Included was a diamond-set tiara with large pear-shaped diamonds (pl. 4). As unlikely as it seems today, this type of grand head ornament, usually signifying European royal or aristocratic rank, was also worn by American elites in the years leading up to World War I. Many New York matrons of the Gilded Age wore their tiaras at the old Metropolitan Opera in what was appropriately dubbed the Diamond Horseshoe. In the Cartier Paris archives there are albums that contain photos of dozens of tiaras designed for American clients during this period—and they were not just made for Americans married to Europeans.

In addition to her tiara, Cartier made Townsend an array of white diamond jewelry that comprised a choker necklace (pl. 39) and a grand *devant de corsage* breast ornament (pl. 5). The overall effect of these glittering white diamonds placed at the bosom, neck, and head would have been similar to that of the jewels worn by royalty of the day, such as Queen Alexandra of England (pl. 32). All of Townsend's pieces were designed

6. View of the Beaux-Arts Townsend mansion in Washington, D.C., now the Cosmos Club, showing some of its neoclassical architectural details

according to Cartier's signature Louis XVI style. The choker is made of interlacing garlands of flowers and foliage; the tiara uses rolling classical scrollwork; and the most spectacular of Townsend's jewels, the breast ornament, is made of sprays of lilies entwined with a garland of roses, in the taste of the late eighteenth century. Remarkably, the jewels coordinated perfectly with the Beaux-Arts style of her mansion on Embassy Row, which had been recently transformed by the New York firm of Carrère and Hastings. The new facade and interior, with its obligatory ballroom, included much neoclassical ornament typical of Louis XVI taste, with swags, medallions, masks, vases, and garlands adorning walls, windows, and doors (pl. 6). The Louis XVI style was so versatile that its applications could range from architecture and decor to the most intricate pieces of jewelry. Townsend's patronage of Cartier must mark one of the rare moments when architecture and jewelry were so perfectly in tune.

As we have seen, Cartier had already established an important client base of rich Americans even before it opened in New York. The most prominent names of the Gilded Age were customers in Paris; members of the Vanderbilt family, for example, appear frequently in the Cartier archives for these years. Consuelo Vanderbilt, Duchess of Marlborough (1877–1964), bought a Fabergé-style clock in 1908 (pl. 47). Her cousin by marriage, Mrs. Cornelius Vanderbilt III (1870–1953), had an array of grand jewelry that

opposite:
7. Mrs. Cornelius Vanderbilt III, ca. 1909, wearing her 1909 Cartier necklace in its original form (see pl. 8 for one of its pendants). She also wears the tiara supplied by Cartier in 1909 and a rose brooch purchased in 1904.

8. *Pendant*

CARTIER PARIS, 1909

This hexagonal pendant was once part of the grand necklace shown in
pls. 7 and 9. [cat. 25]

9. Mrs. Cornelius
Vanderbilt III wearing
the same suite
of Cartier jewels,
photographed by Cecil
Beaton in her Fifth
Avenue mansion, 1941

she is shown wearing in a photograph taken around 1909 (pl. 7). Her unusual necklace with hexagonal pendants (pl. 8) was acquired as a special order from Cartier in 1909. At her bosom she wears a diamond-set rose that Cartier had sold her in 1904. It was an old piece, made in 1855, but its royal provenance outweighed its old-fashioned design — it had been made for Princess Mathilde, scion of the Bonaparte dynasty during the Second Empire. Under her bosom Vanderbilt wears a huge breast ornament, terminating in tassels and fringed to an extent that it is difficult to determine where the diamond fringes stop and the fringes of her dress begin. The crowning touch is a grand "Russian" tiara that gives the wearer added height as well as status. Mrs. Vanderbilt bought it in 1909.[9] Initially scorned by her husband's family as an adventuress and an unsuitable marriage prospect, Grace Vanderbilt rose to become a leader of New York society, and she continued to wear her Cartier jewels at the opera and at parties in her Fifth Avenue mansion until the end of her life (see pl. 9).

Consuelo Vanderbilt's sister-in-law, Mrs. William K. Vanderbilt II (1875–1935, pl. 34), was more readily accepted into the clan despite the fact that she was the daughter of a once-poor Irish immigrant miner who made a fortune in the Comstock Lode. Known as Birdie to her family, Virginia Graham Fair Vanderbilt was born in San Francisco. With her sister, Theresa Fair Oelrichs, she built that city's famous Fairmont Hotel. In 1906 she acquired a grand scroll tiara in the form of a crown set with diamonds and pearls, and in the same year she ordered an impressive diamond necklace of eighteenth-century inspiration with a bow knot at its center.[10] Cartier Paris supplied several of the Vanderbilt women with grand jewelry in those years. In 1909 Virginia Vanderbilt's stepmother-in-law, Anne Harriman Sands Rutherford—confusingly known as Mrs. William K. Vanderbilt, Sr.— ordered two diamond bandeaux, one in a highly original Byzantine design of interlacing ornaments that attached with a string of pearls, and the other made of enormous pear-shaped diamonds.[11] In 1910 she bought a long dress ornament called an *écharpe,* a sort of sash that fixed to the shoulder and looped across the breast.[12] Then she had another made entirely of diamonds, with two large medallions terminating in pear-shaped drops.[13] Other *écharpes* or *aiguillettes* were made for Mrs. Cornelius Vanderbilt and Mrs. Frederick Vanderbilt, suggesting stiff competition between the Vanderbilt wives for the grandest and most avant-garde Cartier jewelry. Unfortunately, none of those innovative designs survive. Most of the Cartier pieces worn by Virginia Vanderbilt that are included in this catalogue date from the 1920s, when her jewelry designs were more conventional for their time (see pl. 69).

Another figure that became one of Cartier's most important customers was Evalyn Walsh McLean (1886–1947), also the daughter of an Irish immigrant miner who struck gold. At the tender age of twenty-three, honeymooning after marrying Edward McLean of the *Washington Post* family, she bought a 94.8-carat white diamond called the Star of East from Cartier for $120,000. On her next trip to Paris, in 1910, Pierre Cartier showed her the famous blue diamond known as the Hope, which, although it was smaller at 45.52 carats, had a glamorous and legendary provenance. As McLean related in her book *Father Struck It Rich,* although she was fascinated by Cartier's telling of the story of the Hope and its curse, she declined to buy the diamond. She changed her mind later in New York when she saw Cartier's new setting, which surrounded the Hope with alternating square and pear-shaped white diamonds, cunningly designed to disguise the irregular shape of the stone (pl. 10). In 1911 she bought the Hope for $154,000, and she wore the diamond proudly throughout her life (see pl. 11).[14] McLean continued to be a significant customer for Cartier New York thereafter. During the Depression years Cartier sold her a diamond-and-ruby bracelet for $135,000. She seemed to have been aiming for all points of the

10. The Hope diamond in its Cartier setting of 1910

compass with her jewelry collection: the bracelet's main diamond was called the Star of the South.[15]

McLean's purchase of great gemstones illustrates another mainstay of the Cartier business model. Around 1917 Pierre Cartier purchased the famous Star of South Africa, a pear-shaped, 47.69-carat diamond, and reset it as a brooch (pl. 12). The 1869 discovery of the stone is credited with having unleashed the South African diamond rush; before it made its way to Cartier it belonged to the Countess of Dudley and J. P. Morgan. Cartier also handled the sale of some of the famous jewels belonging to Prince Felix Youssoupoff in the 1920s.[16] In 1928 Cartier London sold Mrs. E. F. Hutton the so-called Marie Antoinette earrings, featuring pear-shaped diamonds of 14.25 and 20.34 carats from the Youssoupoff collection.[17] From the same source came the famous black pearls sold by Cartier New York to Mrs. Townsend's daughter, Mathilde Townsend Welles, who sold them back to

11. Evalyn Walsh McLean, ca. 1932, wearing the Hope diamond (pl. 10) with a diamond necklace and chain supplied by Cartier New York in 1932

12. *Star of South Africa brooch*

CARTIER NEW YORK, CA. 1917

The 47.69-carat diamond in its pendant brooch setting by Cartier [cat. 52]

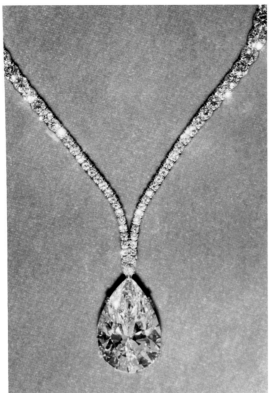

Cartier in 1924 after her husband complained that they looked like decayed oysters.[18] In 1927 Cartier bought the historic Youssoupoff pink diamond, the Tête de Bélier (Ram's Head) of 17.47 carats. Sold to Daisy Fellowes, who had it set into a ring, it was reputed to be the inspiration for Schiaparelli's signature color shocking pink.[19] Perhaps the most famous transaction of all, however, was Cartier New York's sale of the Taylor-Burton diamond. Cartier purchased the then unnamed stone for $1,050,000 in October 1969 and set it into a ring of 69.42 carats. The actor Richard Burton immediately bought it for his wife, Elizabeth Taylor, and it was exhibited by Cartier to large crowds in New York and Chicago before being remade as a necklace and handed over to its new owners (see pls. 13–14).[20]

CARTIER IN NEW YORK

With so many Gilded Age Americans as customers, Alfred Cartier decided to open a store in New York and designated his son Pierre to move there from London. Pierre Cartier's business skills were important to running the enterprise, particularly in negotiating with the millionaires who came to the store. In 1909 there were reputed to be three hundred millionaires living in New York alone.[21] Setting up initially at 712 Fifth Avenue, in 1917 the business moved permanently to 653 Fifth Avenue, where it is housed in a Beaux-Arts mansion (pl. 15). Cartier famously bought the six-story mansion from the industrialist

15. Alexandre Genaille's rendering of Cartier's store on Fifth Avenue, New York, 1920

opposite:
16. View of the main showroom in Cartier's New York store, 1920

Morton F. Plant for $100 plus a double strand of the finest natural pearls, which Mrs. Plant had admired and were worth a million dollars at that time.[22]

The architect Welles Bosworth refitted the interior of the house as a store with references to the Louis XVI style, somewhat reflecting the interiors of the Paris boutique on rue de la Paix (see pl. 16). There was the Blue Room for displaying the most expensive jewels, and the Wedgwood Room for the famous clocks, snuffboxes, and hard-stone animal figures. There were also the Pearl Room and Silver Room. Jules Glaenzer was the principal salesman to whom Pierre Cartier entrusted important clients. In the 1920s and 1930s Glaenzer became a significant host in New York, giving parties where celebrities

17. View of
American Art
Works, Cartier's
New York
workshop, 1930

such as George Gershwin performed for guests from stage and screen, including Paul Whiteman, Noel Coward, Fred and Adele Astaire, Fanny Brice, and Charlie Chaplin.[23] The popular-music composer Richard Rodgers remarked that "Jules and his beautiful young wife, Kendall, had made their series of parties famous for bringing together social registrants, business tycoons and theatrical luminaries in an atmosphere of good talk and music."[24]

Although Cartier New York's stock derived from Paris, a workshop was installed on the fifth floor around 1917. Called the American Art Works, it employed, by 1922, about thirty French workmen who had trained in Paris (see pl. 17). They were supervised by Paul Duru (1871–1971).[25] Later there would be up to seventy jewelers and goldsmiths working with chief stone setter Paul Maîtrejean (1883–1975), the man who reset the Hope diamond. With the coming war, the workshop closed in 1941. After the war it reopened under the operation of an independent contractor, Wors & Pujol. In 1925 a second workshop for making silver and gold objects such as photo frames, commemorative pieces, and vanity cases opened on the other side of 52nd Street. It was called the Marel Works, taken from the names of Pierre Cartier's daughter, Marion, and wife, Elma.[26] The design of the New York–made pieces was under the direction of Frenchmen Alexandre Genaille and Maurice Duvallet.[27] After Duvallet moved on in 1920, Maurice Daudier became the most talented of the New York designers; in the 1940s and 1950s he created pieces for Marjorie Merriweather Post.[28]

At Cartier New York, the process of making a piece of jewelry started with the commission. There were two distinct purposes: a piece could be made either for stock or for a customer as a special order. Most of the stock pieces still came from Paris, but in the case of special orders the client took the lead under Glaenzer's gentle guidance. The whole process was written up in a *Saturday Evening Post* article about Glaenzer in 1948. It is a useful description of how a "fussy" woman might have ordered a ruby-and-diamond bracelet, wanting a variation on the twenty-five already in stock. To paraphrase the article: Having determined that she did not want any of the stock bracelets in the store, the customer gave Glaenzer a rough sketch. He took it to head designer Daudier, who assigned an artist to make a sketch of the bracelet in ink and watercolor. If the lady approved the sketch, it was turned over to the gemologist, who retrieved stones from a huge safe on the sixth floor, the size of "a refrigerator in a butcher's shop" with an electrically controlled door. There he selected gems that matched the size and color of those in the sketch. The stones were arranged on wax and shown to the customer. If she approved, she received a letter stating, "Following your instructions, we are executing the bracelets you ordered. The price will be $22,000 and you may expect delivery in five weeks." Then the stone arrangement on wax and the sketch were sent to the workshop for manufacturing.[29]

CARTIER FOR AMERICANS BETWEEN THE WARS

With the United States emerging as the dominant world power in the years following the First World War, Americans became the leading patrons for Cartier in Paris and London as well as New York. In the interwar years Cartier Paris still led in terms of design and craftsmanship. It supplied the New York store with jewelry, accessories such as vanity cases, and lavishly made clocks, which were inscribed "European Clock and Watch Company" for the American market.

Cartier's designs tended to follow one of two distinct styles during this era. The first produced jewelry in an Art Deco mode. Brilliantly colored, with geometric patterns

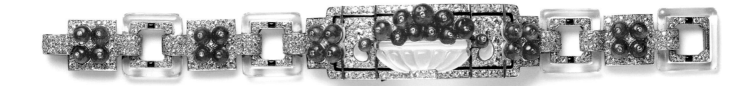

18. *Bracelet*

CARTIER NEW YORK, 1926

Designed in the style of pieces shown at the 1925 Exposition Internationale des Arts Décoratifs et Industriels Modernes, Paris, this piece was made in New York for a member of the Mackay family. [cat. 98]

that often included stylized rather than naturalistic ornamentation, these pieces became synonymous with Cartier in the 1920s. Some characteristic examples (pls. 64–65) were shown in 1925 at the Exposition Internationale des Arts Décoratifs et Industriels Modernes in Paris. A short time later Cartier New York was making pieces in the same style (see pl. 18). The second design mode was the free use of exoticism, a trend that looked in three main directions: China and Japan, ancient Egypt, and, most enduringly, Mughal India. All of these exotic cultural influences would be significant for Cartier's high-society clients of the 1920s and 1930s. Mrs. Cole Porter was particularly fond of Indian-style jewelry and had two bracelets and a clip brooch (pls. 76–78) made to order. Ganna Walska, who also commissioned Indian-style jewelry, acquired Chinese-style pieces as well (see pl. 82, cat. 124), and Mrs. George Blumenthal had an Egyptian sarcophagus vanity case (cat. 89). Exoticism remained a feature of Cartier's jewelry in the postwar era, right up to the end of the twentieth century (see pls. 126, 150).

Concurrent with changes in fashion epitomized by the flappers of the 1920s, jewelry design changed dramatically after World War I. Tiaras, for one thing, fell out of fashion. In the comic novel *Gentlemen Prefer Blondes*, first published in 1925, the gold-digging character of Lorelei Lee is fascinated by her discovery of the tiara, archly declaring it a "new" way to wear diamonds. Always looking for a new angle, she bucks tradition and puts one on backward.[30] In real life, women's shorter hairstyles favored bandeaux, such

19. *Bandeau*
CARTIER PARIS, 1923
Parts of this bandeau diadem can be detached to form two strap bracelets. [cat. 70]

as the one supplied to Mrs. James B. Duke in 1924 (pl. 67); another example, made in 1923, can be taken apart and worn as two bracelets (pl. 19). Like tiaras, bandeaux were made of openwork diamonds but were flexible, more in the form of flat ribbons to be worn low on the forehead (see pl. 58). Long sautoirs, which had originally appeared around 1908, survived as a type of jewelry to be worn with tubular, low-waisted dresses (pl. 66). This was also the era of diamond bracelets, which became increasingly larger by 1930 and were sometimes worn together in numbers—as the movie star Gloria Swanson famously sported hers by Cartier (pls. 20–21).[31] Conversely, the bracelet's counterpart, the diamond-set evening wristwatch, got smaller and smaller, thanks to the tiny movements pioneered by Cartier (see pl. 68). Men's accessories also became an important part of Cartier's production at this time. The man's wristwatch has remained one of Cartier's perennial models. One owned by Al Jolson is an unusual example, with a dial oriented east-west instead of the usual north-south (pl. 22). In addition, the New York workshop made a variety of commemorative pieces for men, such as a tiepin for Fred Astaire commemorating the 1935 musical *Top Hat* (pl. 23), a cigarette case bearing an engraved inscription inside from Douglas Fairbanks (pl. 93), and a silver plaque made for presentation to the actor Alan Mowbray in connection with his role as the agent John Robert Powers in the 1943 movie *The Powers Girl* (pl. 129).

Cartier's principal American clients continued to be the rich and famous of the

20. Gloria Swanson,
ca. 1930, wearing
bracelets supplied
by Cartier in 1930
(pl. 21)

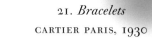

21. *Bracelets*

CARTIER PARIS, 1930

Sold to the actress Gloria Swanson [cat. 150]

22. Single-button chronograph wristwatch
CARTIER NEW YORK, 1924

Sold to the actor Al Jolson in 1931 [cat. 81]

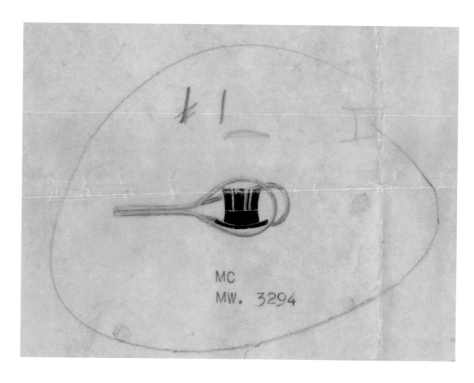

23. Design drawing for Fred Astaire's *Top Hat*–themed tiepin

Gilded Age, such as Virginia Graham Fair Vanderbilt and Evalyn Walsh McLean, but the next generation produced customers from so-called high society, a mixture of the new industrial and mercantile rich mixed with the world of stage and screen—very much as described at Glaenzer's parties. The names of New York society figures are associated with many of the pieces of the interwar years included in this catalogue. From the moneyed classes came Mrs. James B. Duke of the tobacco fortune; Barbara Hutton, the F. W. Woolworth heiress who was married in Paris in 1933 wearing Cartier jewels (pls. 131, 138–140); and Hutton's aunt, Marjorie Merriweather Post, who was then Mrs. E. F. Hutton (pls. 25–26, 85, 98, 114, 121). From the world of finance and newspapers came Mrs. William Randolph Hearst (pls. 68, 75), Mrs. Condé Nast (pl. 86), and Mrs. George Blumenthal, wife of the financier and art collector (pl. 74). From stage and screen came actresses Gloria Swanson and Marion Davies (pls. 58, 84); "opera singer" Ganna Walska, who married Harold F. McCormick, son of the Chicago reaper king (pls. 82, 158); and Mrs. Cole Porter. Cartier's clients also included a growing group of expatriate Americans, prominent among them the decorator and writer Elsie de Wolfe (Lady Mendl), who represented a new type of American woman by making her own fortune rather than marrying one. She lived mainly in France and was voted the world's best-dressed woman by Parisian couturiers in 1935, despite being in her seventies. She was often photographed in magazines in conjunction with her Cartier pieces (see pl. 24).[32] In London, where Lady Cunard ruled society, American-born Lady Granard commissioned substantial pieces of jewelry in the 1930s (see pl. 120). Raised Beatrice Mills

in San Francisco, Granard possessed such enormous pieces from Cartier London that on one occasion, the diarist "Chips" Channon uttered that she "could scarcely walk for jewels."[33] Topping them all, however, was the Duchess of Windsor (pls. 99, 122–127), who was born relatively obscurely in Baltimore yet prompted a king to abdicate his throne. Her jewels by Cartier were an abiding passion for the duke as well as the duchess.

One of the most enduring and loyal American clients for Cartier throughout this period and into the 1960s was Marjorie Merriweather Post (1887–1973).[34] Heir to the Post cereal fortune, she was an active philanthropist and art collector. Although she was raised and lived her life as a staunch Christian Scientist, Post had a long-standing interest in acquiring and wearing jewelry, including historical pieces. In 1971, when she was eighty-four, her "expenditures for clothing and accessories were in excess of $250,000 a year."[35]

25. Giulio de
Blaas's 1929
portrait of Marjorie
Merriweather
Post (then Mrs.
E. F. Hutton) and
her daughter,
Nedenia, shows
Post wearing her
pendant brooch
(pl. 26).

Hillwood Estate,
Museum & Gardens,
51.146

Post's emerald-and-diamond pendant shoulder brooch (pl. 26) is one of the most spectacular Cartier pieces made for an American. Composed of seven carved Indian emeralds, the main one of which dates to the seventeenth century and the Mughal period, it is in the form of a diamond buckle from which the emeralds are suspended as drops. The emeralds are mounted in the most meticulous Cartier manner on a pavé diamond ground with lines of calibré-cut emeralds.[36] The piece was originally made at Cartier London, where it was sold to a Mr. Godfrey Williams in 1924 with an accompanying emerald chain for the enormous price of £10,000.[37] Post, then Mrs. E. F. Hutton, brought the piece to Cartier New York to have it altered in 1928. She is shown wearing the revised version in a 1929 mother-daughter portrait by Giulio de Blaas (pl. 25); in it the brooch becomes the focal point of the composition, nearly upstaging the sitters.

26. *Pendant brooch*

CARTIER LONDON, 1923; ALTERED 1928, CARTIER NEW YORK

Marjorie Merriweather Post was a regular customer at Cartier New York. Her brooch, one of the most spectacular jewels
made in the 1920s, incorporates Indian carved emeralds, one of which dates from the Mughal era. [cat. 71]

From evidence in the Cartier New York archives, Post was continually having her jewelry altered as her tastes changed. In 1936 Cartier altered a diamond-set *devant de corsage*, which she wore as a shoulder brooch in the portrait commemorating her 1929 presentation at court in London, as a clasp for a pearl necklace.[38] Her sapphire-and-diamond collar necklace (pls. 98, 114) was made out of two bracelets by the relatively little-known New York jeweler De Sedles, with a new central section supplied by Cartier in 1937. The Cartier New York archives hold several alternate designs for her amethyst-and-turquoise necklace of 1950 (pl. 121), addressing details right down to the treatment of the gold prong settings. One of the services Cartier provided to its clients was insurance valuation. A valuation of 1941 (by which point she was Mrs. Joseph E. Davies) includes rather surreal photographs of her ears (pl. 27), presumably for estimating the position of earrings during the design process. The insurance of jewelry was a costly business. Post is known to have been so affected by the early years of the Depression that she retired her jewelry into a safety deposit box; with the proceeds saved from the insurance she financed a canteen for the poor.[39]

27. Photographs of Marjorie Merriweather Post's ears included in a Cartier New York insurance valuation of 1941

World War II brought significant changes for Cartier. Production was curtailed in Paris, London, and New York, and two members of the family, Louis and Jacques, died. Despite such upheaval, the styles of the late 1930s generally continued to be used after the war and well into the 1950s. Gold had returned as the metal of choice, replacing platinum for many pieces (with the exception of traditional diamond jewelry) since about 1935. The taste for large, baroque, and sculptural jewelry favored the more plastic qualities of gold. Suites of bracelets and ear clips (see pl. 106) were typical in this era, and after the war gold necklaces appeared. Around 1950 large gold necklaces set with colored gemstones were made for Post and the Duchess of Windsor. In 1953 the leader of European style, Daisy Fellowes, heir to the Singer sewing machine fortune, had a massy gold necklace by Cartier set with diamonds (pl. 104).

The jewels Cartier made for the Duchess of Windsor are among the most remarkable the firm ever produced. Although dispersed at auction after her death in 1987, her collection, which dates mostly from the mid-1930s to 1940 and from 1946 to the early 1960s, has survived almost in its entirety. Many pieces were commissioned by the duke as love tokens marking milestones in their relationship, and some were even designed by him, a fact that has been rarely acknowledged.[40] The Cartier London archives reveal that the duke was very particular about the design of the jewels, however simple.[41]

The duchess's first pieces were relatively small gifts, such as charms for a bracelet, from Cartier London, but by October 1936 King Edward VIII had already put himself on the path to abdication by buying a 19.77-carat emerald ring to celebrate Wallis Simpson's divorce.[42] Like many of the Windsor pieces, it is inscribed inside the platinum shank: "We are ours now 27.X.36." Made a couple of weeks before he declared his intentions to his family, this was the engagement ring for the marriage that caused the king to give up his throne. It was set with a Colombian emerald that was reputed to have been purchased in Baghdad as a much larger stone. When Jacques Cartier decided it was too large for the post-Depression market, it was cut in two.[43] The most iconic piece of jewelry made for the duchess is the flamingo clip brooch of 1940 (pls. 99, 125). Designed under the hand of Jeanne Toussaint (1887–1978, pl. 28), who had been in charge of precious jewelry in the Paris store since the mid-1930s, its fluffed-up plumage is made of calibré-cut emeralds, rubies, and sapphires from existing line bracelets supplied by the duke.[44] After the war Cartier made many more jewels for the duchess. These pieces, all collaborations between the duke, the duchess, and Toussaint, include an amethyst-and-turquoise bib necklace (pl. 122), a panther bracelet (pl. 124), a brooch in the form of a panther sitting on a large star sapphire (pl. 123), and a lorgnette with a tiger for a handle (pl. 126).

The amusing novelty designs of the late 1930s turned out to have an enduring legacy as brooches in the form of flowers, birds, and dogs from the 1950s to the 1990s. The

28. Cecil Beaton's portrait of Cartier's Jeanne Toussaint, 1962

Duchess of Windsor's panthers and tigers of the 1940s and 1950s were, like her flamingo, made under the sway of Toussaint. Although she was not a designer as such, Toussaint dictated the direction of Cartier's designs of this era, particularly the big cats. The panther, tiger, and leopard pieces became a standard for Cartier in the postwar period—see examples belonging to Barbara Hutton from the 1950s and 1960s (pls. 131, 139–140)— and the firm still makes versions of them today. They represent, in a way, a continuation of the exoticism that had been a recurring theme for Cartier since the 1920s. In addition to the cats, the postwar period produced exotic designs in the form of dolphins (pl. 137) and other animals, Indian-style necklaces (pl. 134), and, most sensationally, the massive crocodile and snake necklaces for the Mexican actress María Félix (pls. 132, 150–151). In the 1950s Princess Grace of Monaco had several Cartier brooches in the form of poodles and birds alongside her grand diamond jewelry (pls. 144–149).

Fine jewelry persisted as an important part of Cartier's production throughout the 1950s. More restrained in form than the novelty designs and more feminine, these pieces tended to flatter the wearer rather than overpower her with a grand statement about design. In 1957 the producer Mike Todd gave his new wife, Elizabeth Taylor, a ruby-and-diamond suite of necklace, earrings, and bracelet (pls. 141–143). The enormous pleasure it gave Taylor is evident in stills from a home movie taken in a swimming pool in the south of France (see pl. 29). The discreet, abstract arrangement of the gemstones was typical of the 1950s, and is also visible in the diamond-and-platinum necklace (pl. 145) by Cartier Paris that Princess Grace received as a wedding gift in 1956. It consists of three simple rows of baguette and brilliant-cut diamonds. The princess's engagement ring (pl. 144), also by Cartier Paris, is likewise remarkable in its simplicity. An emerald-cut diamond of 10.47 carats, it appears briefly on the actress's hand in her last movie, *High Society.*

Commemorative and presentation objects have continued as a significant aspect of Cartier's activities. For Christmas of 1962, Jacqueline Kennedy commissioned a handsome paper knife for President John F. Kennedy. As is visible in the design drawings, it is inscribed with both of their initials and the date beneath the presidential seal (see pl. 30). Kennedy's 1961 declaration of America's intention to land on the moon was realized with the Apollo 11 mission of 1969. Cartier commemorated this momentous event with yellow and white gold replicas of the space module with enameled American flags

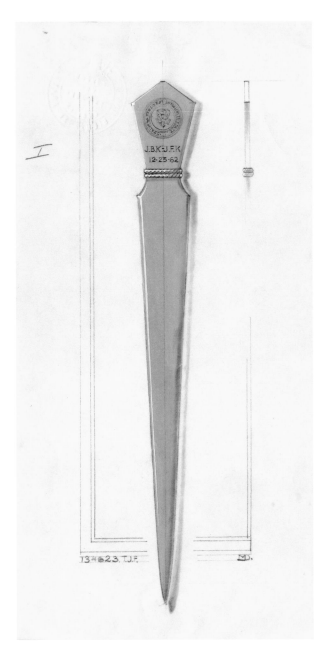

30. Design drawing for a paper knife for President John F. Kennedy, intended as a 1962 Christmas gift from Jacqueline Kennedy

(see pl. 153). They were given to astronauts Neil Armstrong, Buzz Aldrin, and Michael Collins on behalf of the French newspaper *Le Figaro*.

Cartier has never strayed from its commitment to making the most refined jewelry using the highest standards of craftsmanship and the best-quality gemstones. In 1987 a California collector commissioned a version of the Duchess of Windsor's flamingo brooch based on the original designs in the Cartier Paris archives (cat. 277). Created with the expertise of Charles Jacqueau's daughter, it made use of the same calibré-cut technique employed for the colored gemstones in the original and demonstrated that Cartier could still fashion jewelry according to time-honored standards.[45] Cartier's practice of cutting

31. *Orchid necklace*
CARTIER PARIS, 2007

Made as part of the *Caresse d'orchidées* series, this necklace employs a large green beryl for the lip of the orchid and contrasting pink sapphire drops. [cat. 279]

stones to fit the design of its jewelry has been carried over to other projects as well. In the 1990s the firm employed the same type of setting for a series of parrot brooches (see cat. 278).[46] More recently the house embarked on a series of jewelry called *Caresse d'orchidées*.[47] Showing a new interest in sculptural form in jewelry, the line employs Cartier's signature high-quality workmanship as well as unusually colored gemstones. One necklace from the series (pl. 31) employs a carved green beryl for the labellum of the orchid and pink sapphires as contrasting stones. Such work demonstrates that Cartier is still drawing on traditional craftsmanship while appealing to its twenty-first-century patrons' taste for bold form and color.

1. Elsa Maxwell, *How to Do It; or, The Lively Art of Entertaining* (Boston: Little, Brown, 1957), 69.

2. The Cunard account for 1929 includes major purchases of two diamond bracelets, a sapphire-and-diamond necklace, a ruby-and-diamond cluster necklace, an emerald-and-diamond necklace and pendant using the client's stones, and a diamond necklace. In addition to her purchases of smaller items, such as a dressing case, cigarette cases, vanity cases, and stationery, there were numerous repairs: restringing necklaces, rebristling hairbrushes, and remodeling jewelry using Lady Cunard's own stones.

3. Hans Nadelhoffer, *Cartier* (London: Thames & Hudson, 2007), 23. Cartier established its first store in Paris in 1847.

4. Quoted in Diana Scarisbrick, *Ancestral Jewels* (New York: Vendome Press, 1989), 179.

5. Platinum was largely replaced by gold in the mid-1930s, but it continued to be used for fine jewelry.

6. For more on Cartier's connections to couture, see pages 67–71 of this volume.

7. India was an important purveyor of gemstones, and the maharajahs were significant clients for Cartier in Paris as well as London. See Nadelhoffer, *Cartier*, 152–175; Judy Rudoe, *Cartier: 1900–1939* (New York: Metropolitan Museum of Art / Harry N. Abrams, 1997), 31–36.

8. I am grateful to Douglas Reid Weimer for showing me around Mrs. Townsend's Washington mansion, now the Cosmos Club, and sharing the family history with me.

9. Cartier Paris archives. Described as a *diadème russe*, it was made for stock in 1908 and sold to Mrs. Vanderbilt in 1909.

10. Cartier Paris archives. I am grateful to archivist Betty Jais for information on the Vanderbilt purchases.

11. Nadelhoffer, *Cartier*, figs. 86–87.

12. Rudoe, *Cartier*, fig. 52.

13. Nadelhoffer, *Cartier*, fig. 56.

14. Accounts of the diamond's price vary. Evalyn Walsh McLean says, in *Father Struck It Rich*, that it cost $154,000; Nadelhoffer explains that although the selling price was $180,000, McLean received a $26,000 discount for the return of a pearl-and-emerald necklace. McLean, *Father Struck It Rich* (New York: Ishi Press International, 2008), 177; Nadelhoffer, *Cartier*, 318.

15. McLean, *Father Struck It Rich*, 295.

16. Nadelhoffer, *Cartier*, 124.

17. According to the London accounts of October 11, 1928, Mrs. Hutton paid £6,750 (which converted to $32,737). The earrings are now in the collection of the National Museum of Natural History, Washington, D.C. (G5018).

18. Unpublished autobiography of Mathilde Townsend Welles, December 1944, Franklin D. Roosevelt Presidential Library and Museum, Hyde Park, New York. I am grateful to Douglas Reid Weimer for giving me an extract of this typescript. Benjamin Welles, in *Sumner Welles* (Basingstoke, UK: Palgrave Macmillan, 1997), 100, says that the pearls cost $400,000 in 1923. According to Nadelhoffer, they were next purchased in 1924 by Mrs. Peter Goelet Gerry of Washington, D.C., for $400,000 (*Cartier*, 124).

19. Stefano Papi and Alexandra Rhodes, *Famous Jewelry Collectors* (London: Thames & Hudson, 1999), 158. The diamond was reputed to have once belonged to Catherine the Great. The color, now known in the United States as hot pink, was used on the box of Schiaparelli's 1937 scent Shocking. The stone was stolen in 1939 and has not been seen since.

20. Nadelhoffer, *Cartier*, 329.

21. Ibid., 28.

22. Pearls were at their zenith in those years, competing in value with Rembrandt paintings and exceeding that of diamonds. Cartier got the better of this deal with time. The necklace resold for only $151,000 in 1957, by which point natural pearls had lost their value with the advent of cultured pearls. Ibid., 334n13.

23. Edward Jablonski, *Gershwin* (New York: Da Capo Press, 1998), 48.

24. Richard Rodgers, *Musical Stages: An Autobiography* (New York: Da Capo Press, 2002), 121.

25. Rudoe, *Cartier*, 44, fig. 32.

26. Nadelhoffer, *Cartier*, 320n11.

27. Genaille produced the watercolor rendering of Cartier New York that appears as pl. 15.

28. Nadelhoffer, *Cartier*, 330n12.

29. Maurice Zolotow, "Fine Jewels Are His Business," *Saturday Evening Post*, May 8, 1948.

30. Anita Loos, *Gentlemen Prefer Blondes* (1925; repr., New York: Penguin, 1998), 36–37. Lorelei says, "I think a diamond tiara is delightful because it is a place I really never thought of wearing diamonds before. . . . I thought I had almost one of everything until I saw a diamond tiara." However, there are many instances of Americans continuing to wear tiaras well into the middle of the century. Mrs. Cornelius Vanderbilt III, a leader of New York society, was one example (see pl. 9). Barbara Hutton was another. Her many marriages into royalty and nobility—husbands included three princes (one spurious), a count, and a baron—technically earned her the right to wear a tiara; as late as 1947 she commissioned Cartier to make her one using emeralds formerly belonging to the Grand Duchess Vladimir. Hutton's aunt by marriage, Marjorie Merriweather Post (formerly Mrs. E. F. Hutton) made no European royal or aristocratic marriages yet wore tiaras in the 1950s and 1960s, including the one made for Empress Marie Louise of France (now in the collection of the National Museum of Natural History, Washington, D.C.).

31. Swanson wore her bracelets in the movie *Sunset Boulevard* (1950).

32. De Wolfe's fashion triumph was reported in the *New York Herald Tribune*, November 26, 1935. Other Americans on the list were also prominent Cartier clients: Mrs. William K. Vanderbilt, Sr.; Mrs. Ernest Simpson (later the Duchess of Windsor); Mrs. Cole Porter; and the Hon. Mrs. Reginald Fellowes (who is listed as French). For more on photographs of de Wolfe, see pl. 24 in this volume and descriptions in Rudoe, *Cartier*, 30–31. There may have been an understanding between de Wolfe and Cartier; she certainly seems to have received reductions in prices. The Cartier London archives show that on October 9, 1936, she paid £160 for the mother-of-pearl and coral clock shown in pl. 24. It was discounted from £180. She was, however, a good client. In London, on June 17, 1925, she bought a collection of fifty-two pearls for the enormous sum of £11,000. In 1940, after fleeing France, she commissioned a marguerite necklace as a special order in New York, according to the Cartier New York archives.

33. James R. Rhodes, ed., *Chips: The Diaries of Sir Henry Channon* (London: Weidenfeld & Nicolson, 1967), 116.

34. Post is mentioned above with connection to pieces acquired while she was married to her second husband, E. F. Hutton. She reclaimed her maiden name after her fourth (and final) divorce.

35. Nancy Rubin, *American Empress: The Life and Times of Marjorie Merriweather Post* (1995; repr., Lincoln, NE: iUniverse, 2004), 61.

36. The calibré cut was developed at this time for small stones that were usually rectangular and step cut to fit into linear settings.

37. "30 April 1924 One five emld drop and 2 shaped emeralds diamond and emerald loop pendant with diamond collet and emerald long chain £10,000." Cartier London archives. A 1929 photograph in the archives of Hillwood Estate, Museum & Gardens, Washington, D.C., shows Post (in costume as "Juliette" for the Palm Beach Everglades Ball) wearing the emerald sautoir with the brooch suspended from it. The sautoir, shortened in 1941, is now in the collection of the National Museum of Natural History (G5023), along with other of Post's historical pieces, including the above-mentioned Marie Antoinette earrings (G5018) and the Empress Marie Louise necklace (G5019) and tiara (G5021).

38. The 1931 portrait, painted by Giulio de Blaas, is in the collection of Hillwood Estate, Museum & Gardens (51.149).

39. Rubin, *American Empress*, 17.

40. Cartier jewelry played an important role in their relationship from its inception. While on a cruise in

the Mediterranean in 1934, the duke, then Prince of Wales, called on Cartier Cannes in the middle of the night to produce a charm for Mrs. Simpson's bracelet. Greg King, *The Duchess of Windsor: The Uncommon Life of Wallis Simpson* (New York: Citadel Press, 2000), 114. The Cartier Paris accounts of the 1930s, 1940s, and 1950s reveal that it was the duke, rather than the duchess, who commissioned their pieces. The duchess's account tended to be for smaller pieces and repairs.

41. A letter in the Cartier London archives, written by the new Duke of Windsor on August 28, 1937, chides Jacques Cartier for making a clip brooch incorrectly: "You will be careful to note that the WE [the initials of the duchess and duke] on the two designs is incorrect and that they were drawn before I had the center bars of each letter shortened." One of these clips appears in this volume as cat. 184. Although the duke apparently wished this highly personal collection to be broken up after the duchess's death, the auction—which realized just over $31 million—enriched a worthy cause in the Pasteur Institute, Paris. It also ensured the survival of these extraordinary pieces, some of which (pls.

124–125) are on public view in *Cartier and America* for the first time since their sale in 1987.

42. According to documents in the Cartier London archives, Edward VIII purchased the ring on October 31, 1936; the price was £10,000.

43. John Culme and Nicholas Rayner, *Jewels of the Duchess of Windsor* (New York: Vendome Press, 1987), 152. However, Stefano Papi and Alexandra Rhodes question this assertion in *Famous Jewelry Collectors* (London: Thames & Hudson, 1999), 119; they suggest the emerald may have come from a sautoir owned by Nancy Leeds.

44. Culme and Rayner, *Jewels of the Duchess of Windsor*, 171. The Cartier Paris archives include details of the original order from the duke (L5730, October 5, 1940).

45. Suzanne Tennenbaum and Janet Zapata, *The Jeweled Menagerie: A World of Animals in Gems* (London: Thames & Hudson, 2001), 188.

46. Nadine Coleno, *Amazing Cartier* (Paris: Editions du Regard, 2008), 33.

47. Ibid., 115, 123, 125–127.

Courtly Diamonds
THE BELLE EPOQUE, 1899–1918

In 1899, when Cartier moved its Parisian premises to the fashionable rue de la Paix (pl. 33), Americans became increasingly important customers. Vanderbilts, Morgans, and Goulds were part of an international elite that shopped in Paris, crossing the Atlantic twice a year to get dresses fitted at Worth, the great couturier of the era. Their elaborate attire (see pl. 34) was not complete without suites of impeccably made diamond jewelry from Cartier. For the convenience of these customers, the Worth and Cartier stores were situated next to each other on rue de la Paix. Mrs. Richard Townsend of Washington, D.C., heir to a fortune in railroads and coal, had a full complement of Cartier jewelry supplied in 1905–1906. Her tiara, corsage ornament, and choker necklace (pls. 4–5, 39) are all made of white diamonds mounted in platinum and were designed in the Louis XVI revival style. Mrs. William K. Vanderbilt, Sr., also acquired substantial jewelry from Cartier in these years, including a ribbon-bow brooch supplied in 1905 (pl. 38). In commissioning these jewels, both women were following the grand style of the courts of Europe, then undergoing their final moment of splendor in London, Saint Petersburg, and Berlin.

The then queen of England, Alexandra of Denmark, was an important role model for the royal ladies of Europe. She was incomparably beautiful, even in her sixties, and her mode of wearing jewels and dress set the trend for court and grand occasions (see pl. 32). Cornelius Vanderbilt III described the queen as possessing "the world's most perfect shoulders and bosom for the display of jewels."[1] It was to Cartier that King Edward VII turned to supply his queen with a new necklace in 1904.[2] Consuelo Vanderbilt, who became Duchess of Marlborough in 1895, echoed her cousin's words about Alexandra's natural aptitude for wearing jewels.[3] The beautiful and elegant Vanderbilt, one of many rich Americans who married into British and European noble families at the time, followed the queen's lead by draping jewels in copious amounts at her neck and bosom. For Edward VII's coronation in 1902, she wore a choker to accentuate her long neck and ropes of pearls, reputed to have once belonged to Catherine the Great, swagged

32. Queen Alexandra wearing her Cartier necklace of 1904 in an official portrait by François Flameng, 1908
The Royal Collection, RCIN 405360

33. View of
Cartier's shop on
rue de la Paix,
Paris, 1912

across her chest. She and other rich Americans emulated the style of the court in London, which under Edward VII was cosmopolitan and welcoming to Americans.

Cartier's jewelry up to World War I was predominantly neoclassical, a freely adapted version of the Louis XVI revival that was the preferred decorative style of the courts of Europe. Often called the Garland style, it employed swags, tassels, wreaths, and sprays of flowers made of small diamonds exquisitely set in platinum mountings. Evidence of this grand royal taste can be seen in the elaborate scrollwork of the tiara made for Elisabeth, Queen of the Belgians, in 1910 (pl. 41), which is framed at the top by a garland, or row of stylized foliage, and in a 1912 stomacher brooch (pl. 42), which again presents scroll-work from which depend garlands of diamonds. Cartier also used the Louis XVI style for the paneling of its Paris showrooms, which were fitted out like small eighteenth-century salons (see pl. 35).

opposite:
34. Virginia
Graham Fair
Vanderbilt was one
of Cartier's patrons
in the Gilded Age.
She appears in this
1905 portrait by
Giovanni Boldini
wearing the
typically elaborate
dress of the period.

Fine Arts Museums of
San Francisco, gift of
Mrs. Vanderbilt Adams,
67.31.1

From about 1905 Cartier offered a whole range of Russian-style objects, mostly luxury accessories such as desk sets, clocks, and photo frames decorated in enamel. They are very much in the style of Fabergé but display the extraordinary variety of colors and decoration employed by Cartier. Russian-style objects were purchased by prominent Americans such as Anna Gould, who at this point was married to the flamboyant Comte de Castellane (pl. 45), and Nancy Leeds, who became Princess Anastasia, wife of Prince Christopher of Greece (pl. 48). Cartier is even thought to have sold miniature frames in the Fabergé style to the royal family in Saint Petersburg (see pl. 46).[4] In 1908 Consuelo Vanderbilt, newly separated from the Duke of Marlborough, bought a clock decorated in Cartier's characteristic lavender enamel (pl. 47). Cartier even had the hard-stone animal figures so beloved by the Edwardians (pls. 49–51) carved in the same workshops as Fabergé.[5]

With regard to jewelry, white diamonds set in platinum remained the standard until the First World War, but subtle changes took place. Cartier was interested in exploiting the delicacy and lightness of its jewelry to complement the feminine fashions of the day, even when the perennial Louis XVI style started to run out of steam. One new approach was to produce pieces that resembled textiles. A brooch made in 1906 (pl. 53) for Sir Ernest Cassel, banker to Edward VII, demonstrates that Cartier could produce jewelry as delicate as a lace. A different approach, from around 1910, was to make pieces with abstract geometric patterns, executed with astonishing delicacy. Two such examples (pls. 52, 54) were made for Grace Vanderbilt, wife of Cornelius Vanderbilt III. Even white diamond jewelry began to take on a more exotic look. Grace Vanderbilt acquired an extraordinary necklace with suspended hexagonal motifs (see pls. 7–9).[6] With its geometric form and Byzantine references, it looks more like something from the workshops of Louis Comfort Tiffany than Cartier—and perhaps not unintentionally. More radical changes in design occurred just before the outbreak of war in 1914, with startlingly original models inspired by the Russian ballet (see pls. 55–56). These highly stylized jewels, designed by Charles Jacqueau, resonated with Paul Poiret's exotic fashions. With their weighty emeralds and sapphires in geometric settings, they are clearly forerunners to the highly colored designs of the Art Deco era.

1. Leslie Field, *The Queen's Jewels: The Personal Collection of Elizabeth II* (New York: Harry N. Abrams, 1987), 11.

2. The piece was a choker-cum-necklace called a *collier résille*. Flexible and light, it was a remarkably delicate piece of jewelry made up of a simple geometric lattice that gave the effect of a waterfall of diamonds. See Hans Nadelhoffer, *Cartier* (London: Thames & Hudson, 2007), fig. 65.

3. "She had sloping shoulders and her breasts and arms seemed specially fashioned for a fabulous display of glittering jewels." Consuelo Vanderbilt Balsan, *The Glitter and the Gold* (1952; repr., Maidstone, UK: George Mann Books, 1973), 75.

4. Anne Odom, *What Became of Peter's Dream? Court Culture in the Reign of Nicholas II* (Middlebury, VT: Middlebury College Museum of Art; Washington, DC: Hillwood Museum and Gardens, 2003), 57, fig. 26, cat. 62.

5. Judy Rudoe, *Cartier: 1900–1939* (New York: Metropolitan Museum of Art / Harry N. Abrams, 1997), 102.

6. One of the pendants from Vanderbilt's necklace appears as pl. 8 in this catalogue.

36. *Tiara*

CARTIER PARIS, 1902

Made from 759 brilliant-cut and 289 rose-cut diamonds, this tiara was made for the former Adele Grant of New York, who became Countess of Essex in 1893. Renowned for her beauty, she was one of the hundred or so American heiresses who married into the British aristocracy in the decades flanking 1900. [cat. 2]

37. *Tassel pendant*

CARTIER PARIS, CA. 1905

38. *Bow brooch*

CARTIER PARIS, 1905

This tassel-form pendant and ribbon-bow brooch are examples of the Louis XVI or Garland style of the
Belle Epoque. Both are still set in silver (and gold) rather than platinum.
The brooch was sold to Mrs. William K. Vanderbilt, Sr. [cat. 8, 11]

39. *Choker necklace*
CARTIER PARIS, 1906

Made as a special order for Mrs. Richard Townsend of Washington, D.C., this necklace was part of a suite of
grand jewelry in the Louis XVI style (see pls. 4–5). [cat. 12]

40. Stomacher brooch

CARTIER PARIS, 1907

This exceptionally elaborate type of jewelry was made in emulation of eighteenth-century examples that
were intended to ornament the bodice. [cat. 18]

41. *Tiara*

CARTIER PARIS, 1910

This tiara was made for Elisabeth, Queen of the Belgians, after her marriage to Albert I,
who became king in 1909. [cat. 32]

42. *Stomacher brooch*

CARTIER PARIS, 1912

A supreme example of the Garland style, this brooch has three garlands suspended from it. [cat. 38]

43. *Cube clock*

CARTIER PARIS, CA. 1908

The cube clock was one of Cartier's most successful models in the Fabergé style. This one has a minute repeater: when the moonstone button is depressed, it strikes the hour, quarter-hour, or minute. In place of numerals on the dial, letters spell out *BONS SOUHAITS* (best wishes). [cat. 24]

44. *Desk set*

CARTIER PARIS, 1908

This desk set includes a cube clock as well as inkwells and a pen. Each piece is decorated in
Cartier's distinctive color combinations of mauve, green, and gray enamel, bordered in white and featuring
engine-turned patterns. [cat. 22]

45. *Egg-shaped desk clock*

CARTIER PARIS, 1907

This piece was originally sold to Anna Gould, the daughter of American railroad magnate Jay Gould and
ex-wife of the Belle Epoque socialite Compte Boni de Castellane. [cat. 15]

46. *Frames with photographs of Grand Duchesses Tatiana Nikolaevna and Olga Nikolaevna*

CARTIER PARIS, CA. 1910

The photographs of the daughters of Tsar Nicholas II in these frames suggest that Cartier was able to sell Fabergé-style wares even to members of the Russian royal family. [cat. 34]

47. Cube desk clock

CARTIER PARIS, 1908

This clock was sold to Consuelo Vanderbilt, Duchess of Marlborough. [cat. 21]

48. *Frame*

CARTIER PARIS, 1910

Nancy Leeds, who is shown in the picture, commissioned this frame in 1910. Widow of the tin millionaire William B. Leeds, she became Princess Anastasia of Greece in 1920. [cat. 29]

49–51. *Three animal figures: a pig and two bulldogs*

CARTIER, ca. 1905–1912

Cartier retailed carved hard-stone figures that were very similar to those sold by Fabergé.

[cat. 10, 20, 39]

52. *Brooch*

CARTIER PARIS, 1910

Originally a hatpin made for a member of the Rothschild family, this was transformed by Cartier
into a brooch and sold to Mrs. Cornelius Vanderbilt III (pls. 7, 9). [cat. 28]

53. *Lace jabot brooch*

CARTIER PARIS, 1906

This brooch, designed to imitate lace, was sold to Sir Ernest Cassel, financier to King Edward VII.

[cat. 13]

54. *Pendant brooch*

CARTIER PARIS, 1913

Sold to Cornelius Vanderbilt III, this was originally made as a pendant. [cat. 45]

55. *Pendant brooch*
CARTIER PARIS, 1913

56. *Pendant brooch*
CARTIER PARIS, 1912

Both of these brooches were conceived under the powerful influence of the Russian ballet and the
emerging style of Modernism. That on the left was exhibited at Cartier New York in November 1913
as part of the exhibition *Collection of Jewels Created by Messrs Cartier from the Hindoo, Persian, Arab, Russian,
and Chinese.* [cat. 37, 43]

Fashioning New Jewelry
ART DECO, 1918–1937

The period between the wars is often seen as one of Cartier's greatest moments. Producing daring, colorful creations using cabochon and carved emeralds, rubies, and sapphires or coral, onyx, and jade, Cartier embraced modernism as it was characterized at the 1925 Exposition Internationale des Arts Décoratifs et Industriels Modernes in Paris. Richly decorative, the geometric designs are tempered with a measure of figurative ornament and splashes of color that hark back to the Russian ballet influence of the prewar era. The return to peace ushered in the era of the flapper, whose new fashions—including tubular silhouettes and short skirts—required fresh approaches to the design and wearing of jewelry. These came in the form of buckle brooches to accentuate low waists (pls. 62, 73), brooches and pins to secure cloche hats (pl. 70), and dangling pendant earrings to hang below bobbed hair (pl. 71). The actress Marion Davies, who typified the new American woman, was photographed in 1921 wearing an innovative type of jewelry: a bandeau diadem set fashionably low on her brow (pl. 58). The portrait demonstrates how Mrs. James B. Duke would have worn the diamond-and-pearl bandeau (pl. 67) made for her by Cartier New York in 1924.

At the 1925 exposition in Paris, Cartier showed conspicuously not with the jewelers but with the couturiers in the Pavillon de l'Elégance, underlining the continuing attention to fashion that had informed its jewelry production since the early years of the century, when it cemented its close relationship with the couture house of Worth through both proximity and marriage.[1] It was essential to Cartier that its jewelry interact successfully with the fashions of the ruling elites, to a degree that the firm almost completely ignored art movements such as Art Nouveau around 1900 and the hard-edged International Modernism of the 1930s. Cartier's display at the 1925 exposition featured a fully made-up mannequin whose torso, draped as if wearing a silk dress, was adorned

57. Cartier's display at the Exposition Internationale des Arts Décoratifs et Industriels Modernes, Paris, 1925

67

58. Actress Marion Davies, ca. 1921, wearing the bandeau diadem fashionable during the Art Deco period

with a suite of emerald-and-pearl jewelry (pl. 57). Significantly, it showed how Cartier's new jewelry was to be worn: the tiara low on the brow, long pendants at the ears, a large brooch fixed at the bust, and an unusual necklace/shoulder ornament slung across the chest and fastened to the dress at the back.[2] The latter piece, an extreme interpretation of the new jewelry style, demonstrated the possibilities of geometric designs incorporating pearls, diamonds, and brilliantly colored carved Mughal emeralds, a type of stone used frequently by Cartier in the late 1920s and 1930s.

Many of Cartier's principal clients were considered leaders of fashion. Daisy Fellowes launched, according to Jean Cocteau, "more fashions than any other woman in the world."[3] She was always on the best-dressed lists of Parisian couture in the 1930s and was a faithful Cartier client. Part of the new international set sometimes called café society, she was the daughter of a French duke and lived in France and England; her mother, however, was American, the heiress of the Singer sewing machine fortune. In the 1930s Fellowes was the Paris correspondent for *Harper's Bazaar*, in which she expressed her

59. Daisy Fellowes wearing her 1936 "Hindu" necklace (pl. 79) in a portrait by Cecil Beaton, 1936

edgy attitudes toward fashion.[4] Her relationship with Cartier is one of the longest of any patron, stretching from the 1910s to the 1960s, and her famous "Hindu" necklace of 1936 (pl. 79) is nothing short of iconic of the Indian style of jewelry. Her involvement in the design of the piece was extensive. Inspired by a necklace Cartier made for the Maharajah of Patna in 1935, she supplied 783 of her version's 1,029 gemstones herself.[5] Although the Indian style was not new in 1936, her contribution resulted in an unusually full necklace bursting with emeralds, rubies, and sapphires. Fellowes's vision of how the piece would interact with fashion is revealed in a Cecil Beaton photograph that shows her wearing it with her favorite, sequin-embroidered Schiaparelli jacket (pl. 59). Although the necklace was later altered by Fellowes's daughter, Cartier's design drawing of 1936 (pl. 60) shows that it was originally intended to be fastened by a silk cord.

Exoticism was a persistent aspect of Cartier's jewelry and accessories during this era. Objects made in the style of India, ancient Egypt, China, and Japan were seen as alternatives to the more uncompromising aesthetic of Modernism. India was the most

60. Design drawing for Daisy Fellowes's 1936 necklace (pl. 79)

61. Design drawing
for Mrs. Harrison
Williams's 1927
inkwell (pl. 81)

long-lived exotic influence, providing the carved gemstones so loved by Cartier's clients in the 1920s and 1930s. It was the jewelry made in the so-called Tutti Frutti style that Cartier made its own. Made of carved Indian emeralds, rubies, and sapphires, this is the jewelry that was favored by Mrs. Cole Porter, who had suites of bracelets and dress clips fashioned in this distinctive manner (see pls. 76–78). Egypt had inspired a range of jewelry from about 1910, but in the mid- to late 1920s it became popular for accessories as well. The most spectacular example is an Egyptian-style clock (pl. 74) made in 1927 and sold in 1929 to Mrs. George Blumenthal, who also owned an Egyptian sarcophagus vanity case. China, and to a lesser extent Japan, influenced a range of clocks, jewelry, and accessories in the late 1920s, including a Chinese porcelain inkwell mounted in gold (pls. 61, 81) that was produced by Cartier New York for Mrs. Harrison Williams (later Countess Mona Bismarck). Sometimes Cartier mounted whole objects, such as Bismarck's scent bottle of 1926 (pl. 80), while in other cases it incorporated sections of Chinese lacquer, as in a desk clock purchased as a present by William S. Paley (pl. 83).

The 1920s and 1930s were the era of the luxury accessory. Vanity cases were the most typical of the time. Made of gold and decorated with enamel and sometimes gemstones, they were vehicles for lavish decoration (see pls. 90–91). Their gold interior fittings were carefully designed with compartments to hold powder, lipstick, and rouge. Some accessories featured ingenious mechanisms. A cigarette case for Virginia Graham Fair Vanderbilt (pl. 92), made of gold enameled with Persian motifs of leaping deer, has a spring-loaded base; when the user slides back the top, it presents a single cigarette. The extensive range of accessories sold in New York included special orders such as a frame in agate, citrine, and enamel (pl. 85) for Marjorie Merriweather Post, then Mrs. E. F. Hutton (one of several frames made for her by Cartier New York), and a silver traveling cocktail set complete with shaker, lemon squeezer, and tumblers (pl. 96).

1. Louis Cartier married Charles Worth's granddaughter Andrée in 1898; his sister Suzanne married Jacques Worth some years later.

2. Judy Rudoe, *Cartier: 1900–1939* (New York: Metropolitan Museum of Art / Harry N. Abrams, 1997), fig. 269.2.

3. In a 1964 issue of American *Vogue*, James Pope-Hennessy described Fellowes as having "very great beauty, a subtle exquisite barbed sense of humour,

an inborn taste for dress, and a considerable fortune." Quoted in Stefano Papi and Alexandra Rhodes, *Famous Jewelry Collectors* (London: Thames & Hudson, 1999), 158.

4. Judy Rudoe, "The Taste for 'Barbaric Splendour': Daisy Fellowes and Her 'Hindu' Necklace," *Jewellery Studies* 9 (2001): 87.

5. Ibid., 85.

62. *Belt buckle brooch*

CARTIER PARIS, 1922

This brooch was intended as a belt ornament to accent the low-waisted dresses of the 1920s. Designed with dramatic geometric motifs in the Art Deco style, it is set with an octagonal step-cut emerald of 38.71 carats flanked by palmette motifs with cabochon sapphires, emeralds, and diamonds. [cat. 63]

63. *Pendant brooch*

CARTIER PARIS, 1922

A quintessential Art Deco design in its brilliant color and strong form.
The vase can be worn separately on a little cord. [cat. 68]

64. *Bracelet*

CARTIER PARIS, 1924

65. *Bracelet*

CARTIER PARIS, 1925

These bracelets were among the items displayed by Cartier in 1925 at the famous Exposition Internationale
des Arts Décoratifs et Industriels Modernes in Paris. [cat. 76, 84]

66. *Sautoir*

CARTIER PARIS, 1928/1929

This sautoir can be broken down into two bracelets and a shorter necklace. That is the way it must have been
worn in the 1930s, when long, sautoir-type chains were no longer in fashion. [cat. 133]

67. Bandeau

CARTIER NEW YORK, 1924

This piece was once owned by Doris Duke, daughter of American Tobacco Company founder
James B. Duke. Her mother, Nanaline Holt Inman, commissioned this fashionable hair ornament to be worn with
the shorter hairstyles of the 1920s. [cat. 75]

68. *Bracelet watch with cover*

CARTIER NEW YORK, 1927

Watches got smaller following the invention in 1925 of the double-layer Duoplan movement by Jaeger,
the firm that supplied Cartier's watch movements. This example was owned by Millicent Veronica Wilson, who
married William Randolph Hearst, the American press baron, in 1903. [cat. 107]

69. *Fruit-bowl brooch*
CARTIER PARIS, 1925

70. *Cliquet pin*
CARTIER PARIS, 1925

Both of these pieces, sold to Virginia Graham Fair Vanderbilt (pl. 34) in 1925, represent distinct jewelry styles
of the time. The fruit-bowl brooch has the stylized form and brilliant coloring of Art Deco, while the pin shows
the more exotic influence of India in the palm-shaped motif that is made of a piece of Chinese jade.

[cat. 87, 90]

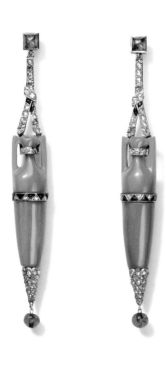

71. *Earrings*

CARTIER PARIS, 1924

72. *Pendant necklace*

CARTIER PARIS, 1922

Brilliantly colored coral, a favorite gemstone of the 1920s, is featured here in two very different treatments.
The vases of the earrings are inspired by ancient Greek pottery, while the form of the pendant is derived from
Chinese amulets. The earrings belonged to Elma Rumsey, wife of Pierre Cartier;
the necklace belonged to Marchioness Curzon of Kedleston, who was born Grace Elvina Hinds,
daughter of the American diplomat Joseph Monroe Hinds. [cat. 69, 78]

73. Scarab buckle brooch

CARTIER LONDON, 1924

Cartier responded enthusiastically to the 1922 discovery of the tomb of Tutankhamun with a range of Egyptian-style pieces, some incorporating ancient fragments, as here. This brooch could be used as a buckle on an enameled gold belt. The blue Egyptian faience on the scarab's wings dates from the second half of the first millennium BCE. Another example of this type of design was acquired by Mrs. Cole Porter. [cat. 80]

74. *Egyptian striking clock*

CARTIER PARIS, 1927

Based on the gate of the Temple of Khons at Karnak, this is the most impressive of Cartier's Egyptian-style objects.
An archival photograph of 1927 (pl. 156) shows it completed in Maurice Couët's Paris workshop.
Two years later, Cartier New York sold the clock to Florence Blumenthal. She was first wife of George Blumenthal,
who headed the Wall Street investment bank Lazard and was a trustee (and later president) of the
Metropolitan Museum of Art, New York. [cat. 113]

75. *Bracelet*

CARTIER NEW YORK, 1927

Made of carved Indian sapphires, this bracelet was sold to Millicent Veronica Wilson,
wife of William Randolph Hearst. [cat. 106]

76. *Strap bracelet*

CARTIER PARIS, 1925

Cartier pioneered its Indian-style jewelry in the 1920s. Made of colorful, carved Indian gemstones,
this type of jewelry is now known as Tutti Frutti. This bracelet is designed as a wavy, diamond-set stem from
which sprout ruby and sapphire leaves and emerald berries. Mrs. Cole Porter, a great fan of Cartier's
Tutti Frutti style, owned this and several other pieces (see pls. 77–78). [cat. 94]

77. *Strap bracelet*
CARTIER PARIS, 1929

78. *Double clip brooch*
CARTIER PARIS, 1935

Both of these pieces belonged to Mrs. Cole Porter. Considered one of the most beautiful women in the world,
Linda Lee Thomas was born in Louisville, Kentucky, and married the famous American composer in 1919.
The double clip brooch was a design typical of the 1930s; the two pieces could be taken apart
and worn separately. [cat. 144, 171]

79. *"Hindu" necklace*
CARTIER PARIS, 1936; ALTERED 1963

Arguably the most famous Tutti Frutti piece made by Cartier, this necklace was created as a special order for
the Hon. Mrs. Reginald Fellowes (pl. 59), daughter of Duc Decazes and Isabelle Singer (heiress to the Singer
sewing machine fortune). Daisy Fellowes commissioned the necklace after she saw one that Cartier designed for
an Indian maharajah in 1935. She supplied many of the gemstones herself. [cat. 177]

80. *Scent bottle*

CARTIER PARIS, 1926

81. *Inkwell*

CARTIER NEW YORK, CA. 1927

Louis Cartier, who was an art collector, encouraged the firm to incorporate exotic art objects into some of its
creations in the 1920s. Cartier mounted both of these Chinese works of art as luxury accessories for
Mona Travis Strader, later Countess Mona Bismarck. In 1926 she married the financier Harrison Williams,
one of the richest men in America. [cat. 103, 121]

82. *Belt*

CARTIER LONDON, 1930

Carved to imitate Qing dynasty coins, these Chinese jade medallions were set with rubies by Cartier London.
The belt was sold to one of Cartier's most loyal clients, the Polish-born Ganna Walska, whose fourth of six
husbands was Harold F. McCormick of Chicago. Her talentless singing apparently inspired the character of
Jean Alexander in *Citizen Kane*. Her great passion was the creation of the exotic gardens at Lotusland, Santa
Barbara; in the 1970s she began to sell off her extensive jewelry collection to finance them. [cat. 149]

83. *Desk clock*

CARTIER PARIS, 1920

Set with a panel of Chinese lacquer, this complex desk clock marks the hours by means of gold numerals that
rotate across the dial and point to the minutes. The clock was given as a present by William S. Paley,
head of the Columbia Broadcasting System (CBS), one of the three major American networks. [cat. 59]

84. *Striking clock*

CARTIER NEW YORK, 1925

This Chinese-style Art Deco clock, set with panels of lacquer, was given as a present by
Mr. and Mrs. Horace Gates Brown. Mrs. Brown was the movie star Marion Davies (pl. 58), the former companion
to William Randolph Hearst. [cat. 95]

85. *Frame with portrait of Marjorie Merriweather Post*

CARTIER PARIS, 1929

Post, then Mrs. E. F. Hutton, commissioned several frames made of precious materials that would complement the colors of each portrait. The use of agate in this example matches Post's brown-accented costume.

[cat. 141]

86. Evening bag

CARTIER PARIS, 1929

The clasp of this handbag, set with carved, leaf-shaped rubies and emeralds, is engraved inside with Mrs. Condé Nast's name and Park Avenue address in case it was mislaid. [cat. 140]

87. *Tank cintrée wristwatch*

CARTIER LONDON, 1929

This watch was sold to Fred Astaire, the multitalented dancer, choreographer, singer, and actor, who gave it to his racehorse trainer, Felix Leach. [cat. 145]

88. *Desk watch*

CARTIER PARIS, 1929

This desk watch was purchased by the movie star Douglas Fairbanks. [cat. 139]

89. *Cigarette box*

CARTIER PARIS, 1929

This silver box was presented to Mr. and Mrs. William K. Vanderbilt, Jr., after their 1928–1929 voyage
around the world on the yacht *Ara*. [cat. 137]

90. *Vanity case*

CARTIER NEW YORK, CA. 1924

91. *Vanity case*

CARTIER NEW YORK, CA. 1926

Two very different styles of vanity case from the mid-1920s. That on the left, with its striped case,
is conservative for its date. It was given by the Duke of Westminster to the designer Coco Chanel.
The example on the right is more boldly ornamented and colorfully Art Deco. The interior is fitted with a mirror
and two lidded compartments, one containing a lipstick holder. [cat. 83, 104]

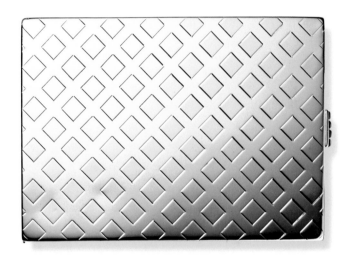

92. *Cigarette case*

CARTIER PARIS, 1932

Decorated with Persian ornament, this case is fitted with a spring system so that a cigarette pops out
as the lid slides back. It was owned by Virginia Graham Fair Vanderbilt (pl. 34). [cat. 162]

93. *Cigarette case*

CARTIER LONDON, 1932

This case was purchased by the actor Douglas Fairbanks and his third wife, Sylvia (Lady Ashley, née Hawkes),
as a gift for Joan Buckmaster, wife of the actor Robert Morley and daughter of Dame Gladys Cooper. [cat. 163]

94. *Cigarette case*

CARTIER PARIS, 1931

Cigarette cases given as presents were often inscribed by the donors. This example, which was sold to the photographer Baron Adolf de Meyer, is engraved with signatures of prominent members of café society, including those of Coco Chanel, Misia Sert, Daisy Fellowes, Peggy Guggenheim, Cécile Sorel, Elsie de Wolfe, and Prince Jean-Louis de Faucigny-Lucinge. [cat. 157]

95. *Cigarette case*

CARTIER LONDON, 1932

Designed in the form of an envelope, complete with enamel stamp, this gold case is addressed in the hand of Winston Churchill to his son, Randolph, for his twenty-first birthday. [cat. 161]

96. *Cocktail set*

CARTIER NEW YORK, CA. 1930

Comprising a shaker, two flasks, a lemon squeezer, and six tumblers, this traveling set fits into a
black leather carrying case. [cat. 155]

The Return to Gold
PRE- AND POSTWAR, 1935–1955

Gold came storming back into fashion for jewelry in the mid-1930s. With the aftermath of the Depression requiring greater economy, along with a shift to a more sculptural type of jewelry, gold came to outshine the more expensive platinum. Although platinum was still used for grand diamond and gem-set jewelry, gold was the metal of choice. American *Vogue* commented on Cartier's booth at the Paris exposition of 1937, "There's a great greed for gold-rich yellow gold and hoards of it. No little gram weight nuggets content this age—your jewel pieces will be huge and affluent."[1] Cartier used gold for bold bracelets with a greater sense of scale and weight, exemplified by a 1938 bangle set with lapis lazuli beads (pls. 100–101) and a 1939 cuff with citrines and amethysts (pl. 102). It continued to be used after the war in an even more baroque manner, resulting in sweeping gestures and large shell motifs (see pl. 103). When destined for the fashion maverick Daisy Fellowes, gold could turn heavy and massive, as in her 1953 necklace set with small diamonds (pl. 104).

Cartier had always employed gold for vanity cases, but now the metal took on a more overt presence. A huge case made in London for the American-born Lady Granard presents a large expanse of gold relieved only by her cipher and clasps in diamonds (pl. 119). Other accessories of this time are more discreet, such as a 1936 cigarette case with sapphires (cat. 175) and a 1946 powder case, randomly set with cabochon rubies, that was sold to the actress Vivien Leigh (pl. 105). Both objects sport a dominant background of polished gold.

Cartier also started selling a new type of gold jewelry: novelty brooches with curious or exotic themes such as a hand holding a rose, influenced by Surrealism and by the revived fashion for sentimental Victorian jewelry. In 1937 the firm introduced enameled gold clips in the form of blackamoors (pl. 110). Intended as fastenings for a dress, these items linked Cartier firmly to the world of fashion. The notorious fashion editor Diana Vreeland wrote about the clips in her memoir: "Have I ever showed you my little

97. Design drawing for the Duchess of Windsor's 1947 bib necklace (pl. 122)

98. Marjorie
Merriweather Post
wearing her 1937
necklace (pl. 114)
in a 1946
portrait by
Frank O. Salisbury

Hillwood Estate,
Museum & Gardens,
51.143

99. The Duke
and Duchess of
Windsor, 1940.
The duchess is
wearing her 1940
flamingo clip
brooch (pl. 125).

blackamoor heads from Cartier with their enameled turbans? Baba Lucinge and I used to wear them in rows and *rows* . . . they were the *chic* of Paris in the later 1930s."[2] Novelty brooches continued through this period; Sioux chief and squaw clips (pls. 108–109) succeeded the blackamoors in 1938, and brooches in the form of exotic birds and flowers in turn succeeded them. The bird brooches became Cartier standards in the postwar era, sometimes with comic results, as with the cowboy duck of 1950 (pl. 111). Despite such whimsical subjects, the war was difficult for Cartier. In a grim scenario reminiscent of the movie *Casablanca*, Louis Cartier died in Lisbon in 1942 while waiting for a visa to the United States, and eleven key members of the Paris staff were imprisoned. Jeanne Toussaint (pl. 28) and Peter Le Marchand integrated subversive patriotic references in their designs; little brooches modeled as caged birds, representing France under the Occupation, prompted the Nazis to interrogate Toussaint.[3] At the end of the war Cartier redesigned the brooches to show a happy bird emerging from the cage, commemorating the Liberation (pl. 112).

Cartier continued to use platinum for high-society grand jewelry. Marjorie Merriweather Post, a client of Cartier New York since the 1920s, continued her patronage in the 1930s with more commissions and alterations to her growing collection of jewelry. In 1936 she had Cartier create a necklace of sapphires and diamonds set in platinum (pl. 114), which she wore for a 1946 portrait (pl. 98). The Virginia-born Phyllis Brand, sister to Lady Astor, was the wearer of an exotic tiara of turquoises and diamonds set in platinum (pl. 113). It was probably made for the 1937 coronation of George VI, for which Cartier made a remarkable total of twenty-seven head ornaments.[4] Also set in platinum are Mrs. Irving Berlin's grand diamond brooch with lustrous cabochon emeralds (pl. 115) and a pair of diamond dress clips that can be attached to a black enameled bangle (pls. 117–118)—an example of the convertibility that is characteristic of Cartier's jewelry. A rose diamond brooch set in platinum (pl. 116), made in 1938, is grander version of Cartier's novelty flowers and also harks back to Victorian jewelry. It was eventually given to Princess Margaret, whose middle name was Rose.

The Duchess of Windsor (pl. 99), who in 1946 had publicly expressed her preference for wearing platinum in the evening, changed tack when she had her famous bib necklace (pls. 97, 122) set in twisted gold only a year later.[5] Probably made in acknowledgment that parties were less formal postwar, this dramatic piece of jewelry marks a continuation of the Indian style that had begun in the 1920s.[6] In 1949 the duchess's jewelry reverted to platinum with a diamond-and-sapphire panther poised atop a Kashmir sapphire of 152.35 carats (pl. 123). This brooch, made for stock by Cartier, is among the earliest examples of the panthers that would become an important part of Cartier's precious jewelry for decades to come. The duchess also owned a 1952 panther bracelet (pl. 124) that is remarkably executed; the body is made in many separate segments so that the piece remains supple in the hand, like a textile. The head can be turned according to the wearer's whim.

1. Quoted in Judy Rudoe, *Cartier: 1900–1939* (New York: Metropolitan Museum of Art / Harry N. Abrams, 1997), 24.

2. Vreeland continued, "When I moved to New York I made arrangements for the Paris Cartier to sell them to the New York Cartier, and all I can tell you is that the race across the ocean . . . was something fierce." Diana Vreeland, *DV* (1984; repr., New York: Da Capo Press, 1997), 53.

3. Hans Nadelhoffer, *Cartier* (London: Thames & Hudson, 2007), 233, 313; *Story of . . . : Memories of Cartier Creations* (Tokyo: Tokyo National Museum, 2009), 114; Nadine Coleno, *Amazing Cartier* (Paris: Flammarion, 2008), 28.

4. Rudoe, *Cartier*, 258.

5. In answer to persistent press questions about the theft of her jewels in England in 1946, the duchess answered angrily, "A fool would know that with tweeds or other daytime clothes one wears gold, and that with evening clothes one wears platinum." Greg King, *The Duchess of Windsor: The Uncommon Life of Wallis Simpson* (New York: Citadel Press, 2000), 380.

6. Cartier would repeat the unusual combination of translucent amethyst and opaque turquoise in a necklace designed for Mrs. Post in 1950 (pl. 121).

100–101. *Bangle*

CARTIER PARIS, 1938

Jewelry of the late 1930s acquired a sculptural boldness for which gold was more appropriate than platinum. The striking design of this bangle is seen here in views of both sides: one with lapis beads and the other with gold. [cat. 191]

102. *Handcuff bracelet*

CARTIER PARIS, 1939

The handcuff form of this bracelet is set with the unusual color combination of amethysts and brown citrines.

[cat. 201]

103. *Bracelet*

CARTIER NEW YORK, CA. 1945

The boldness in Cartier's design continued after the war with large statements such as this swirling baroque bracelet incorporating a shell motif. [cat. 217]

104. *Necklace*

CARTIER PARIS, 1953

Other postwar designs were more static yet still massive. This articulated necklace, made of solid gold decorated
with a feather motif and small diamonds, came from the collection of Daisy Fellowes (pl. 59). [cat. 240]

105. *Powder case*

CARTIER NEW YORK, 1946

This piece was sold to Vivien Leigh, the actress who received one Oscar in 1940 for her performance in *Gone with the Wind* and another in 1952 for *A Streetcar Named Desire*. The case, sprinkled with cabochon rubies, is engraved with the monogram *GL*, the initials *V+L*, and the date 1952, probably referring to Gertrude Lawrence, who let Leigh and her husband, Laurence Olivier, stay in her New York apartment during the 1951–1952 acting season. [cat. 219]

106. *Buckle bracelet and ear clips*

CARTIER NEW YORK, 1948

Designed to resemble a belt, the bracelet, made of fifteen interwoven rows of "laminated gold fabric," is exceptionally supple. [cat. 224]

107. *Orchid brooch*

CARTIER PARIS, 1937

This flamboyant design in the form of an orchid is set with an unusual combination of amethysts and
aquamarines. The gemstones were calibré cut to fit into the compartments and secured with gold claws,
the tops of which have been disguised with tiny dots of colored enamel. [cat. 187]

108–110. *Clip brooches: Sioux, squaw, and blackamoors*
CARTIER PARIS, 1937–1938

Cartier responded to the vogues of the late 1930s by making a succession of novelty clip brooches.
The fashion maven Diana Vreeland owned a pair of blackamoor clips
(the ones shown here were sold to an Indian prince). [cat. 188, 197–198]

111. *Cowboy duck brooch*

CARTIER NEW YORK, CA. 1950

112. Oiseau libéré *brooch*

CARTIER PARIS, 1947

During World War II Cartier designed brooches featuring caged birds that symbolized occupied France.
Once Paris was liberated, the patriotically colored birds emerged joyously from their cages. Cartier continued to
make novelty brooches in a variety of forms, some comic, after the war. [cat. 222, 230]

113. *Tiara*

CARTIER LONDON, 1936

Made for the Virginia-born Phyllis Brand, the sister of Lady Astor, this exotic tiara is designed
with a distinctive Southeast Asian influence. [cat. 181]

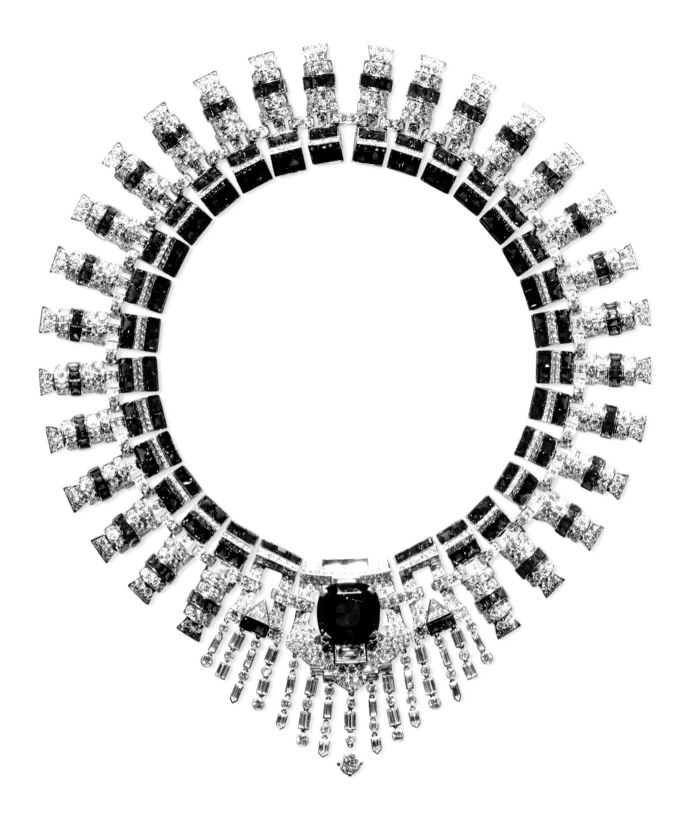

114. *Necklace*

CARTIER NEW YORK, 1937

When her then husband, Joseph E. Davies, was appointed the American ambassador to the Soviet Union,
Marjorie Merriweather Post called on Cartier to transform an existing pair of bracelets into this substantial collar
necklace by adding a central section containing a large sapphire. [cat. 186]

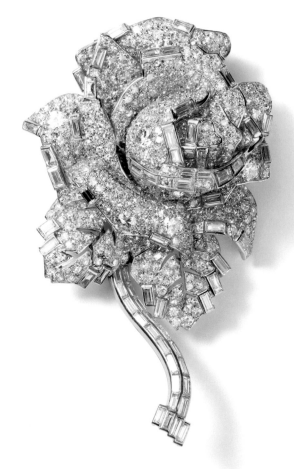

115. *Clip brooch*
CARTIER NEW YORK, 1937

Commissioned as a special order by Mrs. Irving Berlin, this brooch contains particularly fine cabochon and drop emeralds. The daughter of Clarence Mackay (head of the American Telephone and Telegraph Company) and the granddaughter of John Mackay (owner of the Comstock Lode silver mines), Ellin Mackay married the famous American composer against her father's wishes in 1926. [cat. 185]

116. *Rose clip brooch*
CARTIER LONDON, 1938

The British royal family continued to patronize Cartier between and after the wars. This diamond rose brooch was given to Princess Margaret, whose middle name was Rose. The younger daughter of King George VI and Queen Elizabeth, the princess wore this brooch to the 1953 coronation of her sister, Queen Elizabeth II, at Westminster Abbey, London. [cat. 196]

117–118. *Bangle with clip brooches*
CARTIER NEW YORK, 1936

Cartier specialized in jewelry that could be converted for various purposes. This pair of diamond clips
may be worn on a dress or as the terminals of a lacquered bangle. [cat. 174]

119. Vanity case

CARTIER LONDON, 1935

The interior of this unusually large case is fitted with a mirror and four compartments, one for cigarettes. The coroneted monogram *BG* is for Beatrice, Countess of Granard, who was raised in San Francisco as the daughter of the financier and philanthropist Ogden Mills. One of the many American heiresses married to British peers, she wed the eighth Earl of Granard in 1909. [cat. 173]

120. *Necklace*

CARTIER LONDON, 1932

The American-born diarist "Chips" Channon wrote of Lady Granard in 1937 that "she could scarcely walk for jewels." Granard was a regular client of Cartier London and was particularly fond of enormous tiaras, ordering three between 1922 and 1937. This substantial diamond-and-platinum necklace contains an emerald of 143.23 carats. [cat. 164]

121. *Necklace*

CARTIER NEW YORK, 1950

Made as a special order for Marjorie Merriweather Post (then Mrs. Joseph E. Davies), this necklace features
a combination of translucent amethysts and opaque turquoises reminiscent of the Duchess of Windsor's 1947
bib necklace (pl. 122). The drawings for Post's necklace in Cartier's New York archives show alternative schemes
for setting the large amethysts as well as details of the gold prong settings. [cat. 229]

122. *Bib necklace*

CARTIER PARIS, 1947

The Windsors remained loyal Cartier clients throughout their married life. Their commissions were collaborations
with Jeanne Toussaint (pl. 28), who was in charge of fine jewelry in Paris. In this case the duke placed the order
and supplied the stones (except the turquoises), the duchess ensured that it was suitable for her to wear, and
Toussaint directed them toward the Indian-inspired style that persisted into the postwar era. This grand necklace
represents a break with tradition in that it is set in gold rather than the usual platinum. [cat. 220]

123. *Panther clip brooch*

CARTIER PARIS, 1949

One of the first three-dimensional panthers conceived by Jeanne Toussaint, this brooch was made for stock
but sold to the Duke and Duchess of Windsor in 1949. The panther is pavé-set with diamonds and
tiny sapphire cabochons. The Kashmir cabochon sapphire is of 152.35 carats. [cat. 227]

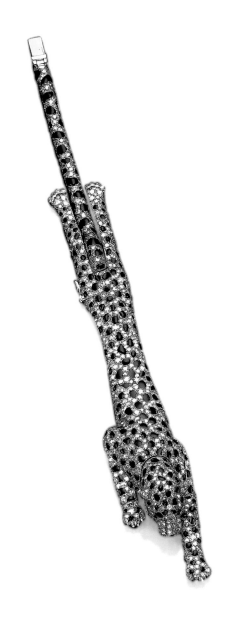

124. *Panther bracelet*

The Duchess of Windsor extended her collection of panthers with this bracelet, set with calibré-cut
black onyx and diamonds and featuring emeralds for eyes. It is articulated in sections so it can be wrapped
around the wrist and the head can even be turned. [cat. 234]

125. *Flamingo clip brooch*
CARTIER PARIS, 1940

This brooch is perhaps the most famous piece of jewelry made for the Duchess of Windsor (pl. 99).
Designed as a special order for the duke with the collaboration of Jeanne Toussaint, it is set with a pavé of
diamonds. The unnaturalistic coloring of the bristling plumage was dictated by the calibré-cut rubies, sapphires,
and emeralds in the necklace and four bracelets the duke supplied for making the brooch. [cat. 204]

126. *Tiger lorgnette*
CARTIER PARIS, 1954

127. *Pug clip brooch*
CARTIER PARIS, 1955

The May 1955 issue of American *Vogue* featured the Duchess of Windsor with her tiger lorgnette in an illustration
by René Bouché. The hinged lorgnette folds out from behind the tiger handle. The duchess famously loved
pugs; the duke bought her the enameled brooch on the right in 1956. [cat. 242, 245]

128. *Five-dial clock*

CARTIER NEW YORK, 1930

Pierre Cartier presented this clock of black onyx, green nephrite, and silver to President Franklin D. Roosevelt on December 20, 1943, in gratitude for the American war effort. The somber, masculine character of the clock must have seemed appropriate for the difficult times. It has five dials showing time zones around the world and bears a French inscription honoring Roosevelt as the architect of "the hour of victory in the world." [cat. 151]

129. *Commemorative plaque*
CARTIER NEW YORK, CA. 1943

This silver plaque was given to the actor Alan Mowbray in recognition of his leading role in the 1943 movie *The Powers Girl.* Mowbray played John Robert Powers, who founded a famous modeling agency in 1923. Several major stars came through the agency, including Grace Kelly. The plaque is signed by Powers and several of the models, known as "the long stemmed American beauties." [cat. 212]

Novelty and Tradition

1950s–1980s

The 1950s to the 1980s was a period of significant change for Cartier. The New York operation changed ownership in 1962, and after Pierre Cartier died in 1964 the family gave up control of the business. All three branches were eventually sold to different buyers, but were brought back together under one owner in 1979. Notwithstanding such changes, Cartier continued its jewelry-making traditions throughout this period. As in the realm of couture, the fine jewelry tradition, whereby pieces were made to exacting standards and tailored to order, was no longer in such high demand. Regardless, it remained the backbone of the business and resulted in restrained and elegant formal pieces for Princess Grace of Monaco and Elizabeth Taylor in the 1950s. The novelty brooches introduced in the prewar years continued in the form of birds, poodles, flowers, and a range of other whimsical forms. In the 1960s and 1970s Cartier fused these very different approaches, producing necklaces for the Mexican actress María Félix that were made in the tradition of precious jewelry but with an imaginative sense of theatricality.

The exoticism that had been a presence in Cartier's jewelry since the 1920s persisted throughout this era. A gold necklace set with turquoises and diamonds (pl. 134) updates the Indian style that had inspired a necklace for the Duchess of Windsor in 1947 (pl. 122). Panthers, meanwhile, had featured in Cartier's jewelry beginning in the 1910s. Jeanne Toussaint (pl. 28), in charge of fine jewelry since 1933, advanced a new generation of three-dimensional panther jewelry that started with commissions for the Duchess of Windsor: panther brooches of 1948 and 1949 (pl. 123) and a panther bracelet of 1952 (pl. 124). Tiger jewelry, a variation on the panthers, was made over the years for Barbara Hutton (pl. 131), who had been a client of Cartier since the first of her seven marriages in 1933. Hutton was a highly discerning buyer of jewelry with a penchant for high-quality gemstones. She had Cartier recut the 40-carat Pasha diamond in the late 1930s and reset

130. Official 1959 portrait of Princess Grace of Monaco wearing her 1956 engagement ring, 1953 necklace, and 1955 clip brooches attached to her tiara (pls. 144–146)

131. Barbara
Hutton in 1960
wearing her 1957
tiger clip brooch
(pl. 139)

the Grand Duchess Vladimir's emeralds as a tiara/necklace in 1947.[1] Her superb jade ring (pl. 138) was an early Cartier acquisition.[2] In 1957 she commissioned a tiger brooch (pl. 139), followed by a pair of earrings in 1961 (pl. 140) and a matching bracelet in 1962.[3] Set with yellow diamonds and onyx stripes, the drooping cat form was derived from the limp ram's skin suspended from the insignia of the Order of the Golden Fleece.[4]

Hollywood movie stars had been patrons of Cartier since the 1920s. The bracelets of Gloria Swanson (pls. 20–21), the vanity cases of Mary Pickford and Vivien Leigh (pl. 105), and the watches and accessories of Fred Astaire and Stewart Granger (pls. 87, 152) were among the many pieces supplied by Cartier to actors. Elizabeth Taylor received a remarkable suite of ruby-and-diamond jewelry from Mike Todd in 1957 (pls. 29, 141–143). The necklace has pointed motifs that are distantly related to those of the Indian-style bib pieces, but the overall effect is one of elegance and restraint.

Grace Kelly wore her diamond engagement ring (pl. 144) on the set of her last film, the 1956 movie *High Society*, before she became Princess of Monaco. The ring is a 10.47-carat diamond in the emerald cut, the most challenging to execute and requiring the highest quality of diamonds. Princess Grace received much Cartier jewelry from Prince Rainier (see pl. 3). Her diamond necklace of 1953 (pl. 145) has three rows of brilliant diamonds alternating with baguettes, demonstrating the refinement and elegance for which Cartier's fine jewelry is famous. She wore it in an official portrait with three diamond-and-ruby brooches (pl. 146) executed in the colors of Monaco and mounted as a tiara (see pl. 130).[5] For less formal occasions she acquired a range of novelty brooches. She had a number of bird brooches (pls. 148–149) and more than one poodle brooch (pl. 147). The princess was fond of poodles, having brought her pet poodle with her when she traveled to Monaco for her wedding in 1956.

132. *Leaf-shaped ear clips*
CARTIER PARIS, 1967; ALTERED 1976

These Indian-inspired earrings were owned by the Mexican actress María Félix. [cat. 270]

133. María Félix
in 1975 wearing
her 1967 emerald
ear clips and 1975
crocodile necklace
(pls. 132, 150)

By contrast with Princess Grace's collection, Cartier's jewelry for María Félix (pl. 133), the biggest star of the golden age of Mexican cinema, is daring and exotic in design yet retains the firm's standards of craftsmanship and fine gemstones. The design of a pair of leaf-shaped emerald ear clips (pl. 132) is clearly derived from Indian Mughal motifs.[6] The settings are rendered invisible by beads of green enamel that have been applied to each of the gold prongs that hold the emeralds. In 1968 Félix commissioned a serpent necklace from Cartier Paris. The impressive result (pl. 151) is a completely articulated snake made of platinum and white gold and encrusted with 178.21 carats of diamonds. Its back is enameled for comfort. In 1975 Cartier created another massive necklace for Félix in the shape of two crocodiles (pl. 150). Modeled after a live baby crocodile supplied by the actress, the reptiles' bodies are made of 524.9 grams of gold; one is covered with 1,023 fancy yellow diamonds, while the other is adorned with 1,060 circular-cut emeralds.[7] These extraordinary orders proved that Cartier was still the master of the fine jewelry tradition, and that it could stretch the boundaries of design when working in concert with an inspired patron.

1. Stefano Papi and Alexandra Rhodes, *Famous Jewelry Collectors* (London: Thames & Hudson, 1999), 182–186.

2. She apparently had this ring made to match a jade bead necklace. Ibid., 187.

3. For a drawing of the bracelet, see *Story of . . . : Memories of Cartier Creations* (Tokyo: Tokyo National Museum, 2009), 175. The complete set is illustrated in Papi and Rhodes, *Famous Jewelry Collectors*, 189.

4. Although it seems to have had no direct significance for Hutton, the Order of the Golden Fleece is the leading order of chivalry in Europe.

5. The brooches were given to Princess Grace by the Société des Bains de Mer de Monaco. *Nice Matin*, April 21, 1956.

6. The earrings were originally set with a row of diamonds at the outer edges and were later owned by Doris Duke.

7. *Story of . . .* , 185.

134. *Bib necklace*

CARTIER PARIS, 1955

Set with turquoises and diamonds, this necklace shows Cartier's continuing exotic theme.
With society changing in the 1950s, jewelry became less formal; being set in gold, this example could be worn in
the day as well as the evening. [cat. 243]

135. *Blue rose clip brooch*
CARTIER PARIS, 1959

This stylized, three-dimensional rose is one of the few Cartier pieces made with an invisible setting.
Patented by Cartier in 1933, the setting completely hides the mount that holds the stones. [cat. 256]

136. *Bracelet*

CARTIER NEW YORK, CA. 1960

Made of sapphires and diamonds, this bracelet shows a growing interest in the 1960s in setting stones
without much evidence of their metal mounting. [cat. 259]

137. *Dolphin bangle*
CARTIER PARIS, 1969

This flamboyant and exotic dolphin was made as special order. It is set with 1,028 brilliant-cut diamonds and has emeralds for eyes. [cat. 273]

138. *Ring*

CARTIER PARIS, 1934

Barbara Hutton, heiress to the Woolworth retail fortune, was extremely discerning about her jewelry and
gemstones, enjoying them as works of art. She was introduced to jade as a girl at the San Francisco store Gump's.
This 37.67-carat jade cabochon of exceptional quality is set above a line of contrasting calibré-cut rubies.
The ring may have been acquired to match a jade necklace that Hutton's father gave her
for her wedding in 1933. [cat. 167]

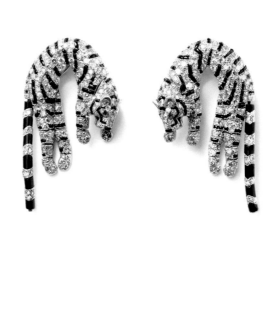

139. *Tiger clip brooch*
CARTIER PARIS, 1957

140. *Tiger ear clips*
CARTIER PARIS, 1961

Cartier augmented its famous panther jewelry with designs in the form of other big cats.
The firm made this tiger brooch and pair of ear clips for Barbara Hutton. Set with yellow diamonds and onyx,
the drooping forms resemble the ram's skin suspended from the insignia of the Order of the Golden Fleece.
The head, legs, and tail of the brooch are articulated. [cat. 255, 264]

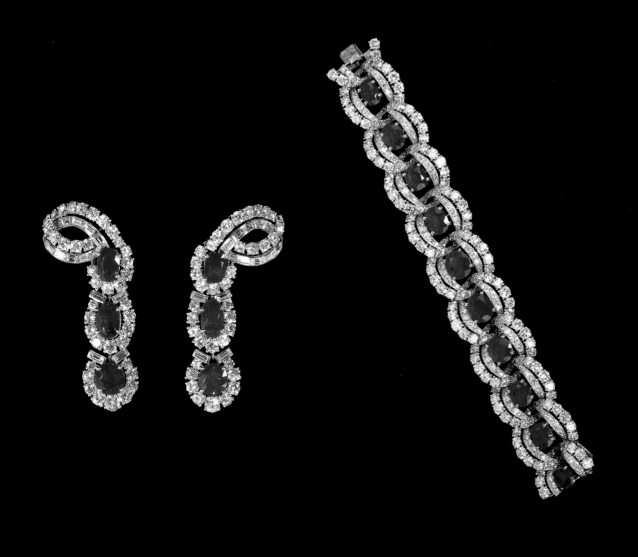

141–143. *Earrings, bracelet, and necklace*
CARTIER PARIS, 1951

This suite of ruby-and-diamond jewelry was given to Elizabeth Taylor by her husband, Mike Todd, in 1957
(see pl. 29). The pointed bib form of the necklace derives from Indian models, yet the whole suite has the
elegance and sophistication that marks Cartier's precious jewelry of the 1950s. [cat. 231–233]

144. *Engagement ring*
CARTIER PARIS, 1956

Made for Grace Kelly's engagement to Prince Rainier of Monaco, this ring was worn by the film star
in her last movie, *High Society.* It is set with a 10.47-carat emerald-cut diamond. [cat. 251]

145. *Necklace*

CARTIER PARIS, 1953

This grand necklace of brilliant and baguette diamonds was a wedding gift to Princess Grace of Monaco.
Its relative simplicity was the mark of Cartier's precious jewelry of the 1950s, which was intended to complement
the wearer rather than make a huge statement. [cat. 239]

146. *Set of clip brooches*

CARTIER PARIS, 1955

Owned by Princess Grace, these three brooches could be worn together or separately.
They could also be mounted on a frame as a tiara (see pl. 130). [cat. 246]

147. *Poodle brooch*
CARTIER LONDON, CA. 1960

148. *Bird brooch*
CARTIER PARIS, CA. 1955

149. *Bird brooch*
CARTIER LONDON, 1956

Princess Grace had a great fondness for poodles; one traveled with her to Monaco when she married
Prince Rainier in 1956. In contrast to her grand diamond jewelry, these dog and bird brooches represent the
more informal and personal style of pieces designed for daytime wear. [cat. 247, 249, 260]

150. *Crocodile necklace*

CARTIER PARIS, 1975

Legend has it that the Mexican movie star María Félix appeared at Cartier's rue de la Paix store with a baby
crocodile as a model for this necklace. The result was a dramatic, masterly creation that could be worn as two
brooches or as a necklace. Each crocodile is made of articulated gold sections. One is set with 1,023 yellow
diamonds and has emeralds for eyes; the other has 1,060 emeralds and ruby eyes. [cat. 275]

151. *Snake necklace*
CARTIER PARIS, 1968

Another special order for María Félix, this necklace, set with 2,473 diamonds, marks the culmination of Cartier's work in modeling animals for jewelry. When handled, the necklace mimics the slitheriness and weight of a real snake with hundreds of individual sections that are hinged internally. To enhance the sensation of snakeskin and protect the wearer, the inside segments of the necklace are enameled. [cat. 272]

152. *Brush set*

CARTIER LONDON, 1966

Made of gold with the initials *SG* applied in lapis lazuli, this dressing set was supplied to the actor
Stewart Granger. [cat. 267]

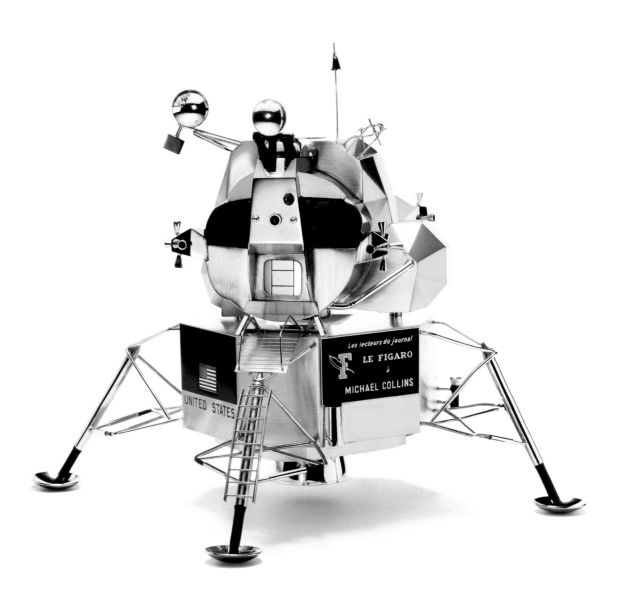

153. *Replica of Apollo 11 lunar module*
CARTIER PARIS, 1969

Cartier has had a thriving business in commemorative pieces. Cartier Paris made three 18-carat gold
models of the lunar module, which were presented by *Le Figaro* newspaper to the three Apollo 11 astronauts
during their postflight tour. This model was given to Michael Collins. [cat. 274]

4579

Mystery Clocks

Cartier's mystery clocks, whose platinum-and-diamond hands appear to float around the dial with no apparent mechanism, were the largest and most elaborate works of art made by the firm. Constructed with a host of precious and semiprecious materials, including rock crystal, onyx, gold, platinum, and diamonds, they are to Cartier what the Easter eggs are to Fabergé. With their myriad components and decorative finishes, the objects were so complex to make that they could take up to a year to complete. The earliest examples, conceived around 1912, were of modest proportions with rectangular cases made of rock crystal. In the 1920s they became larger, and some were embellished with jade sculptural figures.

The mystery that Cartier never meant to reveal was that each hand of the clock was embedded in a flat disk of glass or rock crystal with a concealed, notched edge; this was driven by gears running from a movement hidden in the base. The objects were conceived by the ingenious clockmaker Maurice Couët, whom Cartier put in charge of a Paris workshop owned by the firm in 1919 (see pl. 156). Employing approximately thirty workers, Couët's shop produced clocks of all kinds as well as vanity cases.[1]

The designs for the mystery clocks (supplied by Cartier's chief designer at the time, Charles Jacqueau) varied, but there were five principal types. Model A, featuring a rock crystal case, was the earliest (see pls. 154, 157); J. P. Morgan, Jr., bought an example in 1913. The second type, with a central axle and a dial that was often hexagonal in shape (pls. 155, 159), was made from 1920 to 1931. The third type is the *écran* or screen clock, whose rectangular form is decorated top and bottom with horizontal friezes of jade or moonstone, giving the pieces a very modern Art Deco appearance (cat. 101). The screen clocks were made from 1923 to 1954. Six larger rock crystal *portique* clocks, based on the form of a Shinto shrine gate, were produced between 1923 and 1925. One example was sold to Mrs. Harold F. McCormick, the singer Ganna Walska, in 1923 (pl. 158). Like the jewelry designed by Jacqueau in those years, many of the mystery clocks display a distinctive element of exoticism. This could be demonstrated in the overall form, as in the Japanese-inspired *portique* clocks, or in the ornamental details, such as the Asian decorative motifs on the bases of certain examples.

154. Design drawing for a Model A mystery clock

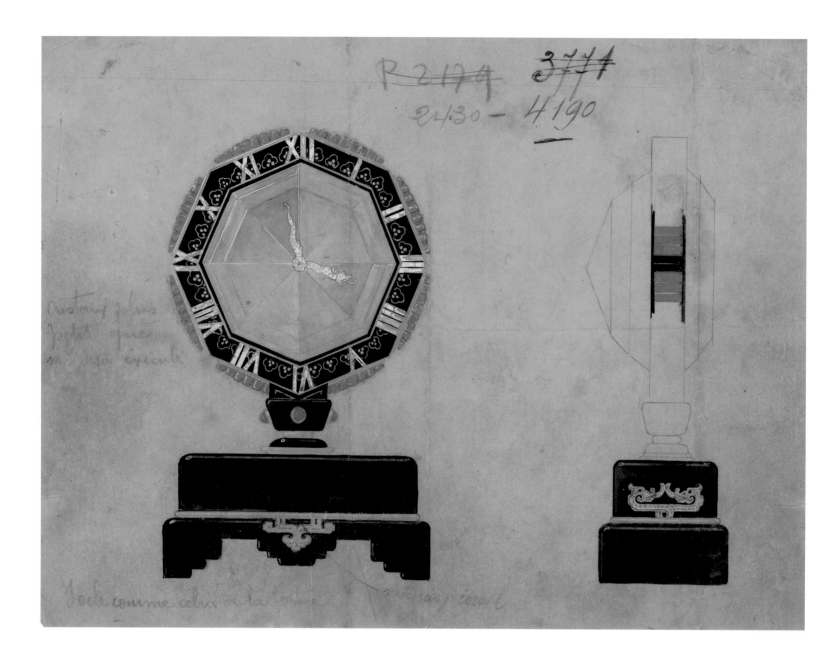

155. Design
drawing for a
single-axle
mystery clock

Last of all came the figural clocks, the most elaborate of the genre. They often incorporate antique Chinese figures, usually made of jade, and were in production from 1922 to 1931. The Mandarin duck clock (pl. 160) was the earliest of this series. Made in 1922, it includes a Chinese jade figure of a duck that is studded with rubies and dates from around 1800. It was followed in 1925 by the carp clock with the retrograde hand (pl. 161). Although the carp is not technically a mystery clock, it has an intriguing movement that involves the hour hand springing back when it reaches the VI at the far right of the dial. The chimera clock (pl. 162) was made for sale in New York by Couët's Paris workshop in 1926. The figure is a piece of antique agate and the dial is citrine. The mystery clock with the goddess Kuan Yin (pl. 164), the last of the series of twelve and the most

148

elaborate of all, was made by the Couët workshop in 1931. A white jade figure of Kuan Yin is elevated on a nephrite pedestal behind the clock's hexagonal rock crystal dial. Flanking them is a jade chimera and a pearl-studded coral branch in a white jade vase. The movement, which strikes the hours, is concealed in the onyx base.

156. View of Maurice Couët's workshop in Paris, where Cartier's clocks were made, 1927

1. Hans Nadelhoffer, *Cartier* (London: Thames & Hudson, 2007), 271. This account is largely based on Nadelhoffer's chapter on mystery clocks.

157. *Model A mystery clock*

CARTIER PARIS, 1914

The first Model A mystery clock was sold by Cartier in 1912. Set in a transparent cage of rock crystal, the platinum-and-diamond hands seem to float in midair. The secret is that each is set into a flat disk of glass with a hidden, toothed edge. These disks are driven by two vertical racks concealed in the sides of the clock, which are in turn driven by the movement in the base. [cat. 48]

158. Portique *mystery clock*

CARTIER PARIS, 1923

Sold to Mrs. Harold F. McCormick (Ganna Walska), this clock was the first in a series of six in the form of a
Shinto shrine gate (*portique*) that were made between 1923 and 1925. [cat. 72]

159. *Mystery clock with single axle*

CARTIER PARIS, 1920

This is one of the very first single-axle mystery clocks produced by Cartier. [cat. 60]

160. *Mandarin duck mystery clock*

CARTIER PARIS, 1922

Between 1922 and 1931 Cartier made twelve mystery clocks, the most ambitious of their kind, mounted with jade
or hard-stone figures. This, the earliest, features a jade duck set with rubies. [cat. 64]

161. *Carp clock with retrograde hand*
CARTIER PARIS, 1925

Although it is not strictly a mystery clock, this piece — the third in the series of twelve figural clocks —
has an hour hand that springs back when it reaches the VI at far right. The jade carps are Chinese,
dating from the eighteenth century. [cat. 86]

162. *Chimera mystery clock*

CARTIER NEW YORK, 1926

Made in Couët's Paris workshop, this piece—like many of Cartier's clocks—was marked by the
European Watch and Clock Company for sale in New York. With an agate chimera standing on a nephrite base
decorated with coral frogs, it was sixth in the series of twelve figural clocks. [cat. 99]

163. Le Ciel *mystery clock*

CARTIER NEW YORK, 1928

With hands in the form of streaking comets, this unusual mystery clock depicts the night sky scattered
with diamond stars. The dial is supported by jade fish decorated with coral and onyx in an overflowing
fountain of rock crystal. [cat. 131]

164. *Striking mystery clock with deity*

CARTIER PARIS, 1931

The largest and last of the grand figural mystery clocks displays a nineteenth-century jade figure of Kuan Yin on a nephrite plinth. The onyx base edged with enameled gold contains the chiming movement. [cat. 159]

157

Catalogue of the Exhibition

This list is arranged chronologically and reflects the most complete information available at time of publication. Cartier's branch of sale, if known, precedes the creation date; inscriptions and provenance are documented whenever possible. Dimensions are provided in centimeters.

1. *Hair ornament*
Cartier Paris, 1902
Diamonds and platinum
7 x 14.2 cm
Sold to Lila Vanderbilt Sloane
(Mrs. William Field)
Cartier Collection, HO 25 AO2

2. *Tiara* (pl. 36)
Cartier Paris, 1902
Diamonds, silver, and gold
8.1 x 20.2 cm
Sold to Adele Grant,
Countess of Essex
Cartier Collection, HO 08 AO2

3. *Fern brooches*
Cartier Paris, 1903
Diamonds and platinum
18.5 x 4 cm (each of two
brooches)
Sold to Sir Ernest Cassel
Cartier Collection, CL 114 AO3

4. *Frame in the form of a
miniature camera*
Cartier Paris, 1904
Yellow gold, white gold, pink
gold, ruby cabochons, pearls,
enamel, and wood
10.5 x 3 x 3.9 cm
Cartier Collection, OV 10 AO4

5. *Scent bottle*
Cartier Paris, 1904
Jade, turquoise, diamonds,
platinum, and gold
5.4 x 4.2 x 1.5 cm
Provenance: J. P. Morgan
Cartier Collection, FK 13 AO4

6. *Seated bulldog*
Attributed to Cartier, ca. 1904
Smoky quartz, gold, sapphires,
baroque pearl, and olivine
6.6 x 3.6 x 5.2 cm
Cartier Collection, AN 11 CO4

7. *Seated rabbit*
Cartier, ca. 1904
Amethyst, silver, diamonds,
and ruby cabochons
3.6 x 2.1 x 3.9 cm
Cartier Collection, AN 12 CO4

8. *Bow brooch* (pl. 38)
Cartier Paris, 1905
Diamonds, silver, and
rhodium-plated gold
4 x 5.1 cm
Sold to Anne Harriman Sands
Rutherfurd (Mrs. William K.
Vanderbilt, Sr.)
Cartier Collection, CL 92 AO5

9. *Tiara* (pl. 4)
Cartier Paris, 1905
Diamonds and platinum
9.8 x 14.6 cm
Sold to Mary Scott
(Mrs. Richard Townsend)
Cartier Collection, HO 09 AO5

10. *Seated pig* (pl. 49)
Cartier, ca. 1905
Rhodonite, gold, and diamonds
4.1 x 3.1 x 7.1 cm
Cartier Collection, AN 16 CO5

11. *Tassel pendant* (pl. 37)
Cartier Paris, ca. 1905
Diamonds, gold, and silver
10.5 x 5.6 cm
Cartier Collection, PE 20 C05

12. *Choker necklace* (pl. 39)
Cartier Paris, 1906
Diamonds and platinum
5.4 x 33 cm
Sold to Mary Scott
(Mrs. Richard Townsend)
Cartier Collection, NE 39 A06

13. *Lace jabot brooch* (pl. 53)
Cartier Paris, 1906
Diamonds, platinum, and gold
17.1 x 6.5 cm
Sold to Sir Ernest Cassel
Cartier Collection, CL 144 A06

14. *Rose-and-lily corsage ornament* (pl. 5)
Cartier Paris, 1906
Diamonds and platinum
19.5 x 29 cm
Sold to Mary Scott
(Mrs. Richard Townsend)
Cartier Collection, CL 134 A06

15. *Egg-shaped desk clock* (pl. 45)
Cartier Paris, 1907
Silver, enamel, silver gilt, gold, diamonds, platinum, and clock movement
8.1 x 6 x 6 cm
Sold to Anna Gould, Comtesse de Castellane, later Duchesse de Talleyrand
Cartier Collection, CCI 04 A07

16. *Head ornament*
Cartier Paris, 1907
Diamonds, pearls, and platinum
3.4 x 13.4 cm
Provenance: Princess Marie Bonaparte
Cartier Collection, HO 26 A07

17. *Lozenge-shaped brooch*
Cartier Paris, 1907
Diamonds and platinum
3.8 x 3.8 cm
Cartier Collection, CL 99 A07

18. *Stomacher brooch* (pl. 40)
Cartier Paris, 1907
Diamonds, sapphires, and platinum
21 x 12.9 cm
Cartier Collection, CL 292 A07

19. *Vase-shaped clock*
Cartier Paris, 1907
Silver, silver gilt, enamel, gold, platinum, diamonds, sapphire, and clock movement
15 x 7 x 5.8 cm
Cartier Collection, CCI 01 A07

20. *Seated bulldog* (pl. 50)
Cartier, ca. 1907
Smoky quartz, gold, and diamonds
6.6 x 5.5 x 4 cm
Cartier Collection, AN 08 C07

21. *Cube desk clock* (pl. 47)
Cartier Paris, 1908
Silver, enamel, agate, gold, diamonds, and platinum
10.5 x 8.1 x 4.2 cm
Sold to Consuelo Vanderbilt, Duchess of Marlborough
Cartier Collection, CDS 19 A08

22. *Desk set* (pl. 44)
Cartier Paris, 1908
Silver, silver gilt, enamel, sapphires, gold, platinum, diamonds, clock movement, and glass
8.3 x 18.5 x 12 cm
Cartier Collection, DI 24 A08

23. *Tiara*
Cartier Paris, 1908
Diamonds, pearls, and platinum
5 x 13.5 cm
Cartier Collection, HO 03 A08

24. *Cube clock* (pl. 43)
Cartier Paris, ca. 1908
Silver, enamel, agate, moonstone, gold, diamonds, platinum, clock movement, and glass
In place of numerals on dial:
BONS SOUHAITS
7.9 x 5.7 x 4.9 cm
Fine Arts Museums of San Francisco, gift of Mrs. Clarence Postley

25. *Pendant* (pl. 8)
Cartier Paris, 1909
Diamonds and platinum
11.9 x 4.7 cm
Sold to Grace Wilson
(Mrs. Cornelius Vanderbilt III)
Cartier Collection, CL 269 A09

26. *Pendant watch*
Cartier Paris, 1909
Diamonds, platinum, pink gold, watch movement, glass, and enamel
L. 69 cm (chain), 3.3 x 3.1 cm (pendant)
Sold to Nellie Melba; sold to Prince Felix Youssoupoff in 1912
Cartier Collection, WN 11 A09

27. *Bow brooch*
Cartier Paris, 1910
Diamonds and platinum
2.2 x 7.2 cm
Cartier Collection, CL 306 A10

28. *Brooch* (pl. 52)
Cartier Paris, 1910
Diamonds, sapphires, and platinum
DIAM. 4.2 cm
Sold to Grace Wilson
(Mrs. Cornelius Vanderbilt III)
Cartier Collection, CL 202 A10

29. *Frame* (pl. 48)
Cartier Paris, 1910
Pink gold, green gold, sapphires, pearls, and engraved rock crystal
Monogram on front: *WBL*
32 x 24 cm
Sold to Nonnie May ("Nancy") Stewart Worthington
(Mrs. William B. Leeds)
Cartier Collection, PF 15 A10

30. *Necklace*
Cartier Paris, 1910
Diamonds, sapphires, pearls, and platinum
L. 44.3 cm (necklace), H. 13 cm (pendant)
Provenance: Mary Scott
(Mrs. Richard Townsend)
Cartier Collection, NE 16 A10

31. *Pendant watch*
Cartier Paris, 1910
Pearls, diamonds, platinum, watch movement, and glass
Monogram in center of case: *CHE*
3.3 x 2.8 cm (case)
Cartier Collection, WN 07 A10

32. *Tiara* (pl. 41)
Cartier Paris, 1910
Diamonds and platinum
5.5 x 13.8 cm
Provenance: Elisabeth, Queen of the Belgians
Cartier Collection, HO 02 A10

33. *Collection of mignonette clocks*
Cartier Paris, ca. 1910
Silver gilt, gold, enamel, diamonds, agate, clock movement, and glass
Approx. 5 x 3.7 x 2.6 cm (each of eleven clocks)
The Lindemann Collection

34. *Frames with photographs of Grand Duchesses Tatiana Nikolaevna and Olga Nikolaevna* (pl. 46)
Cartier Paris, ca. 1910
Silver, enamel, gold, ivory, and photographs
DIAM. 5.1 cm (each of two frames)
Provenance: Russian royal family; Marjorie Merriweather Post (Mrs. Joseph E. Davies)
Hillwood Estate, Museum & Gardens, bequest of Marjorie Merriweather Post, 1973, 11.54.1–2

35. *Necklace*
Cartier Paris, 1911
Pearls, diamonds, and platinum
L. 45 cm
Cartier Collection, NE 05 A11

36. *Lozenge-shaped brooch*
Cartier Paris, 1912
Diamonds, sapphires, pearls, and platinum
3.8 x 4.6 cm
Sold to a member of the Rothschild family
Cartier Collection, CL 249 A12

37. *Pendant brooch* (pl. 56)
Cartier Paris, 1912
Sapphires, diamonds, platinum, and gold
7.4 x 4 cm
Cartier Collection, CL 197 A12

38. *Stomacher brooch* (pl. 42)
Cartier Paris, 1912
Diamonds and platinum
5 x 3.1 x 6.8 cm
Cartier Collection, CL 122 C12

39. *Standing bulldog* (pl. 51)
Cartier, ca. 1912
Agate, gold, pearl, and olivine
6 x 3.1 x 6.8 cm
Cartier Collection, AN 17 C12

40. *Cigarette case*
Cartier Paris, 1913
Gold, rock crystal, enamel, diamonds, platinum, and onyx
9.2 x 4.4 x 1.8 cm
Sold to Lucy Work
(Mrs. Peter Cooper Hewitt)
Cartier Collection, CC 80 A13

41. *Comet clock*
Cartier Paris, 1913
Rock crystal, gold, enamel,
diamonds, platinum, and clock
movement
DIAM. 9.5 cm
Cartier Collection, CS 08 A13

42. *Egyptian-style pendant*
Cartier Paris, 1913
Diamonds, onyx, and platinum
5 x 4.9 cm
Cartier Collection, NE 01 A13

43. *Pendant brooch* (pl. 55)
Cartier Paris, 1913
Emeralds, diamonds, pearls, onyx,
and platinum
9.7 x 3.6 cm
Cartier Collection, CL 183 A13

44. *Pendant brooch*
Cartier Paris, 1913
Jade, turquoise, sapphires, pearl,
diamonds, and platinum
12.3 x 4 cm
Cartier Collection, CL 193 A13

45. *Pendant brooch* (pl. 54)
Cartier Paris, 1913
Diamonds and platinum
9.8 x 2.9 cm
Sold to Cornelius Vanderbilt III
Cartier Collection, CL 277 A13

46. *Vanity case*
Cartier Paris, 1913
Pink gold, yellow gold, enamel,
platinum, diamonds, onyx, pearls,
and mirror
7.2 x 4.5 x .9 cm
Provenance: Marguerite Séverine
Philippine Decazes de Glücksbierg,
Princesse de Broglie, later
Daisy Fellowes
Cartier Collection, VC 85 A13

47. *Desk clock*
Cartier Paris, 1914
Silver, enamel, platinum,
diamonds, gilt metal, clock
movement, and glass
DIAM. 7.9 cm
Sold to Madeleine Talmage Force
(Mrs. John Jacob Astor IV)
Cartier Collection, CDS 62 A14

48. *Model A mystery clock* (pl. 157)
Cartier Paris, 1914
Rock crystal, agate, enamel, gold,
diamonds, platinum, sapphires,
and clock movement
13 x 8.5 x 5 cm
Sold to Count Greffulhe
Cartier Collection, CM 19 A14

49. *Tiara*
Cartier Paris, 1914
Blackened steel, diamonds,
rubies, and platinum
4.1 x 14.6 cm
Sold to Suzanne Mathilde Irma
Prets (Mrs. Michel Marghiloman)
Cartier Collection, HO 11 A14

50. *Tiara*
Cartier Paris, 1914
Diamonds, onyx, pearls, platinum,
and enamel
4.3 x 14.6 cm
Cartier Collection, HO 27 A14

51. *Motorist necessaire*
Cartier New York, ca. 1917
Wood, gold, enamel, clock
movement, glass, and leather
10.6 x 20 x 8.6 cm
Provenance: Vanderbilt family
Cartier Collection, TC 06 C17

52. *Star of South Africa brooch*
(pl. 12)
Cartier New York, ca. 1917
Diamonds and platinum
APPROX. 13 x 8.5 cm
Provenance: Earl of Dudley
Private collection

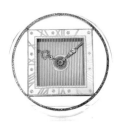

53. *Desk clock*
Cartier Paris, 1918
Rock crystal, gold, enamel, diamonds,
platinum, and clock movement
DIAM. 8.5 cm
Sold to Nonnie May ("Nancy")
Stewart Worthington
(Mrs. William B. Leeds)
Cartier Collection, CDS 84 A18

54. *Flower-basket corsage brooch*
Cartier New York, 1918
Diamonds, pearls, and platinum
9.5 x 7.4 cm
Cartier Collection, CL 256 A18

55. *Serpent necklace*
Cartier Paris, 1919
Diamonds and platinum
19.7 x 12.3 cm
Cartier Collection, NE 20 A19

56. *Yin-yang pendant necklace*
Cartier Paris, 1919
Onyx, diamonds, emeralds,
rubies, platinum, gold, enamel,
and silk
L. 31.5 cm
Cartier Collection, NE 19 A19

57. *Bangle*
Cartier Paris, 1920; altered 1928,
Cartier New York
Platinum, emeralds, diamonds,
and onyx
7.2 x 6.9 cm
Cartier Collection, BT 107 A20

58. *Desk clock*
Cartier Paris, 1920
Gold, enamel, ebonite, silver,
glass, rubies, diamonds, platinum,
and clock movement
8 x 8 cm
Sold to Consuelo Vanderbilt,
Duchess of Marlborough
Cartier Collection, CDS 87 A20

59. *Desk clock* (pl. 83)
Cartier Paris, 1920
Gold, enamel, lacquer, ebonite,
gilded metal, clock movement,
and glass
DIAM. 9.2 cm
Provenance: William S. Paley
Cartier Collection, CS 10 A20

60. *Mystery clock with single axle*
(pl. 159)
Cartier Paris, 1920
Yellow gold, enamel, ebonite,
citrine, diamonds, platinum,
white gold, and clock movement
12 x 8.5 x 4.2 cm
Cartier Collection, CM 16 A20

61. *Bracelet*
Cartier Paris, 1921
Coral, emeralds, pearls,
diamonds, and platinum
2 x 17 cm
Sold to Daisy Fellowes
(Hon. Mrs. Reginald Fellowes)
Cartier Collection, BT 44 A21

62. *Bazuband bracelet*
Cartier Paris, 1922
Diamonds and platinum
14 x 22.3 cm
Sold to Sir Dhunjibhoy Bomanji
Cartier Collection, BT 08 A22

63. *Belt buckle brooch* (pl. 62)
Cartier Paris, 1922
Emeralds, sapphires, diamonds,
and platinum
4.4 x 8.9 cm
Siegelson, New York, F4122

64. *Mandarin duck mystery clock*
(pl. 160)
Cartier Paris, 1922
Gold, platinum, jade, citrine,
onyx, diamonds, rubies,
and enamel
27 x 15 x 10 cm
Sold to Sir Robert Abdy
The Lindemann Collection

65. *Mystery clock with single axle*
Cartier Paris, 1922
Onyx, gold, enamel, rock crystal,
diamonds, platinum, and clock
movement
19.6 x 9 x 4.5 cm
Cartier Collection, CM 02 A22

66. *Pendant brooch*
Cartier Paris, 1922
Emeralds, onyx, diamonds, and
platinum
15.1 x 4.2 cm
Sold as a cliquet pin to Anne
Harriman Sands Rutherfurd
(Mrs. William K. Vanderbilt, Sr.)
in 1920
Cartier Collection, CL 138 A22

67. *Pendant brooch*
Cartier Paris, 1922
Coral, onyx, diamonds, platinum,
and emerald
13.4 x 3.4 cm
Sold to Virginia Graham Fair
(Mrs. William K. Vanderbilt, Jr.)
Cartier Collection, CL 258 A22

68. *Pendant brooch* (pl. 63)
Cartier Paris, 1922
Coral, onyx, diamonds, and
platinum
13.1 x 6.1 cm
Cartier Collection, CL 259 A22

69. *Pendant necklace* (pl. 72)
Cartier Paris, 1922
Onyx, coral, pearls, diamonds,
emerald, platinum, and silk cord
18.5 x 3 cm (pendant)
Sold to Grace Elvina Hinds
Duggan, Marchioness Curzon
of Kedleston
Cartier Collection, NE 03 A22

70. *Bandeau* (pl. 19)
Cartier Paris, 1923
Diamonds and platinum
7.5 x 13.4 cm
Cartier Collection, HO 05 A23

71. *Pendant brooch* (pl. 26)
Cartier London, 1923; altered 1928,
Cartier New York
Emeralds, diamonds, platinum,
and enamel
20.3 x 5.1 cm
Provenance: Marjorie Merriweather
Post (Mrs. E. F. Hutton)
Hillwood Estate, Museum &
Gardens, bequest of Marjorie
Merriweather Post, 1973. 17.75

72. Portique *mystery clock*
(pl. 158)
Cartier Paris, 1923
Rock crystal, onyx, gold, enamel,
diamonds, platinum, coral, and
clock movement
35 x 23 x 13 cm
Sold to Ganna Walska
(Mrs. Harold F. McCormick)
Cartier Collection, CM 09 A23

73. *Vanity case*
Cartier Paris, 1923
Onyx, gold, enamel, coral,
emeralds, diamonds, platinum,
and mirror
5.8 x 4.2 x 1 cm
Sold to Virginia Graham Fair
(Mrs. William K. Vanderbilt, Jr.)
Cartier Collection, VC 01 A23

74. *Set of ashtrays*
Cartier Paris, ca. 1923
Agate, onyx, silver, silver gilt,
jade, and coral
7 x 9.5 x 8 cm
Provenance: Florence Meyer (Mrs.
George Blumenthal)
Cartier Collection, SA 03 C23

75. *Bandeau* (pl. 67)
Cartier New York, 1924
Diamonds, platinum, and pearl
5.3 x 13.2 cm
Provenance: Nanaline Holt Inman
(Mrs. James B. Duke);
Doris Duke
Cartier Collection, HO 28 A24

76. *Bracelet* (pl. 64)
Cartier Paris, 1924
Coral, enamel, mother-of-pearl,
gold, diamonds, and platinum
1.8 x 18 cm
Cartier Collection, BT 90 A24

77. *Cliquet pin*
Cartier Paris, 1924
Emeralds, onyx, diamonds, and
platinum
8.1 x 1.3 cm
Sold to Mona Travis Strader
(Mrs. Harrison Williams), later
Countess Mona Bismarck
Cartier Collection, CL 95 A24

78. *Earrings* (pl. 71)
Cartier Paris, 1924
Coral, emeralds, onyx, diamonds,
and platinum
7.2 x .9 cm (each of two earrings)
Provenance: Elma Rumsey
(Mrs. Pierre Cartier)
Cartier Collection, EG 35 A24

79. *Egyptian-style vanity case*
Cartier Paris, 1924
Coral, mother-of-pearl, lapis
lazuli, onyx, ancient Egyptian
faience, diamonds, gold,
platinum, enamel, and mirror
9.3 x 4.5 x 2 cm
Sold to François Coty
Cartier Collection, VC 64 A24

80. *Scarab buckle brooch* (pl. 73)
Cartier London, 1924
Ancient Egyptian faience, smoky
quartz, enamel, diamonds,
emeralds, platinum, and gold
5 x 13 cm
Cartier Collection, CL 32 A24

81. *Single-button chronograph
wristwatch* (pl. 22)
Cartier New York, 1924
Gold, watch movement, glass,
and leather
Engraved on back of case:
To Johnny from Al Jolson
DIAM. 3.2 cm (case)
Sold to Al Jolson in 1931
Cartier Collection, WWC 09 A24

82. *Vanity case*
Cartier Paris, 1924
Coral, turquoise, onyx, gold, enamel,
diamonds, platinum, mirror, and
wood panels inlaid with mother-of-
pearl, coral, turquoise, lapis lazuli,
malachite, azurmalachite, and agate
6.5 x 11 x 1.7 cm
Cartier Collection, VC 67 A24

83. *Vanity case* (pl. 90)
Cartier New York, ca. 1924
Gold, enamel, diamonds, platinum,
and mirror
8.4 x 4.1 x 3 cm
Provenance: Duke of Westminster;
Coco Chanel
Cartier Collection, VC 39 C24

84. *Bracelet* (pl. 65)
Cartier Paris, 1925
Coral, onyx, diamonds, and
platinum
1.7 x 18 cm
Cartier Collection, BT 05 A25

85. *Brooch*
Cartier New York, 1925
Coral, emerald,
platinum, and enamel
4.8 x 3.8 cm
Cartier Collection, CL 262 A25

86. *Carp clock with retrograde hand*
(pl. 161)
Cartier Paris, 1925
Gray jade, obsidian, rock crystal,
gold, mother-of-pearl, pearls,
coral, emeralds, diamonds,
platinum, lacquer, enamel, and
clock movement
23 x 23 x 11 cm
Cartier Collection, CS 11 A25

87. *Cliquet pin* (pl. 70)
Cartier Paris, 1925
Jade, enamel, rubies, diamonds,
and platinum
9.4 x 2.3 cm
Sold to Virginia Graham Fair
(Mrs. William K. Vanderbilt, Jr.)
Cartier Collection, CL 244 A25

88. *Clock*
Cartier New York, 1925
Lapis lazuli, jade, mother-of-
pearl, enamel, gold, silver, and
clock movement
8.5 x 13.5 x 2.5 cm
Sold to Clarence H. Mackay
Cartier Collection, CDB 02 A25

89. *Eygptian sarcophagus
vanity case*
Cartier Paris, 1925
Bone, enamel, gold, emeralds,
sapphires, diamonds, platinum,
and mirror
15 x 4 x 3.2 cm
Sold to Florence Meyer
(Mrs. George Blumenthal)
Cartier Collection, VC 70 A25

90. *Fruit-bowl brooch* (pl. 69)
Cartier Paris, 1925
Onyx, emerald, rubies, diamonds,
platinum, and enamel
3.4 x 5.2 cm
Sold to Virginia Graham Fair
(Mrs. William K. Vanderbilt, Jr.)
Cartier Collection, CL 06 A25

91. *Horus brooch*
Cartier Paris, 1925
Ancient Egyptian faience,
emerald cabochon, coral, onyx,
diamonds, platinum, gold, and
enamel
4.5 x 7.1 cm
Cartier Collection, CL 263 A25

92. *Sautoir*
Cartier New York, 1925
Emeralds, diamonds, platinum,
and pearls
L. 75.1 cm
Cartier Collection, NE 42 A25

93. *Scarab buckle brooch*
Cartier London, 1925
Ancient Egyptian faience,
diamonds, onyx, citrines, rubies,
emeralds, platinum, and gold
5.5 x 12.4 cm
Cartier Collection, CL 264 A25

94. *Strap bracelet* (pl. 76)
Cartier Paris, 1925
Sapphires, rubies, emeralds, onyx,
diamonds, platinum, and enamel
3.8 x 19.5 cm
Sold to Linda Lee Thomas
(Mrs. Cole Porter)
Cartier Collection, BT 110 A25

95. *Striking clock* (pl. 84)
Cartier New York, 1925
Silver, nephrite, lacquer, gold,
onyx, enamel, clock movement,
and glass
Inscription on back: *To Arnold
from Marion and Horace*
27 x 18 x 14 cm
Sold to Marion Davies
(Mrs. Horace Gates Brown)
Cartier Collection, CDB 01 A25

96. *Scent bottle*
Cartier Paris, 1925
Jade, gold, sapphire, and enamel
6.2 x 4.5 x 2.5 cm
Provenance: Vanderbilt family
Cartier Collection, FK 11 A25

97. *Paperweight*
Cartier, ca. 1925
Gold, agate, and enamel
Inscription on top: *ALVA*
8.9 x 6.5 x 2 cm
Provenance: William K.
Vanderbilt, Jr.
Cartier Collection, DI 14 C25

98. *Bracelet* (pl. 18)
Cartier New York, 1926
Diamonds, rubies, rock crystal,
onyx, platinum, gold, and enamel
18.6 x 2 cm
Sold to a member of the
Mackay family
Cartier Collection, BT 54 A26

99. *Chimera mystery clock* (pl. 162)
Cartier New York, 1926
Agate, nephrite, citrine, gold,
onyx, enamel, coral, diamonds,
platinum, pearls, emerald
cabochons, and clock movement
17 x 13.8 x 7.5 cm
Cartier Collection, CM 23 A26

100. *Clock with Fo dogs*
Cartier Paris, 1926
Rock crystal, ebony, lapis
lazuli, coral, mother-of-pearl,
pearls, gold, enamel, diamonds,
platinum, rubies, emeralds,
sapphires, and clock movement
18 x 22 x 6 cm
Cartier Collection, CDB 12 A26

101. Ecran *mystery clock*
Cartier New York, 1926
Onyx, moonstone, enamel, gold,
rock crystal, diamonds, platinum,
and clock movement
14 x 10 x 6 cm
Cartier Collection, CM 12 A26

102. *Pendant earrings*
Cartier New York, 1926
Jade, enamel, rubies, diamonds,
platinum, and gold
4.9 x 1.5 cm (each of two earrings)
Cartier Collection, EG 25 A26

103. *Scent bottle* (pl. 80)
Cartier Paris, 1926
Coral (nineteenth-century
Chinese snuff bottle), ebonite,
gold, pearl, diamonds, platinum,
mother-of-pearl, and enamel
8.7 x 4.4 x 3.4 cm
Sold to Mona Travis Strader
(Mrs. Harrison Williams), later
Countess Mona Bismarck
Cartier Collection, FK 19 A26

104. *Vanity case* (pl. 91)
Cartier New York, ca. 1926
Gold, enamel, jade, onyx,
diamonds, platinum, and mirror
13.9 x 3.3 x 1.2 cm
Cartier Collection, VC 25 C26

105. *Bowl*
Cartier Paris, 1927
Jade, lapis lazuli, gold, enamel,
and ruby
4.8 x 5.5 x 5.5 cm
Provenance: Florence Meyer (Mrs.
George Blumenthal)
Cartier Collection, OV 04 A27

106. *Bracelet* (pl. 75)
Cartier New York, 1927
Sapphires, emeralds, diamonds,
and platinum
2.5 x 18.5 cm
Sold to Millicent Veronica Wilson
(Mrs. William Randolph Hearst)
Cartier Collection, BT 77 A27

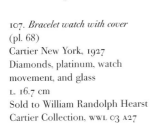

107. *Bracelet watch with cover*
(pl. 68)
Cartier New York, 1927
Diamonds, platinum, watch
movement, and glass
L. 16.7 cm
Sold to William Randolph Hearst
Cartier Collection, WWL 03 A27

108. *Brooch*
Cartier New York, 1927
Diamonds, emerald, onyx, enamel,
and platinum
2.4 x 7.6 cm
Cartier Collection, CL 190 A27

109. *Chinese vase brooch*
Cartier New York, 1927
Lapis lazuli, rubies, diamonds,
platinum, onyx, and enamel
4 x 4.9 cm
Cartier Collection, CL 47 A27

110. *Chinese vase vanity case*
Cartier Paris, 1927
Gold, emerald, sapphire, onyx,
coral, diamonds, platinum,
enamel, and mirror
9 x 5.9 x 2.5 cm
Cartier Collection, VC 68 A27

111. *Cliquet pin*
Cartier New York, 1927
Emeralds, diamonds, enamel, and
platinum
4.9 x 1.7 cm
Cartier Collection, CL 83 A27

112. *Desk clock*
Cartier Paris, 1927
Jade, onyx, coral, lacquer, gold,
enamel, diamonds, platinum,
clock movement, and glass
11.4 x 9.5 x 3.8 cm
Siegelson, New York, F7091

113. *Egyptian striking clock* (pl. 74)
Cartier Paris, 1927
Mother-of-pearl, lapis lazuli, coral,
gold, silver gilt, emerald, cornelian,
enamel, and clock movement
24 x 15.7 x 12.7 cm
Sold to Florence Meyer
(Mrs. George Blumenthal)
Cartier Collection, CDB 21 A27

114. *Lotus-flower deity brooch*
Cartier Paris, 1927
Ancient Egyptian faience, onyx,
diamonds, platinum, emeralds,
rubies, and enamel
5.1 x 3.6 cm
Cartier Collection, CL 161 A27

115. *Mystery clock with single axle*
Cartier Paris, 1927
Obsidian, ebonite, rock crystal,
coral, onyx, gold, enamel,
diamonds, platinum, and clock
movement.
13.9 x 8.6 x 4.2 cm
Provenance: Queen Victoria
Eugenia of Spain
Cartier Collection, CM 25 A27

116. Portique *gravity clock*
Cartier Paris, 1927
Nephrite, jade, onyx, gold, coral,
diamonds, platinum, rubies,
enamel, and clock movement
23 x 12.1 x 7 cm
Provenance: Barbra Streisand
Cartier Collection, CS 14 A27

117. *Temple brooch*
Cartier Paris, 1927
Diamonds and platinum
4 x 1.5 cm
Cartier Collection, CL 44 A27

118. *Vanity case*
Cartier Paris, 1927
Mother-of-pearl, gold, enamel,
cornelian, hard stones, nephrite,
jade, sapphire, ruby, diamonds,
platinum, and mirror
9.3 x 5.3 x 2 cm
Cartier Collection, VC 37 A27

119. *Vanity case*
Cartier Paris, 1927
Sapphires, emeralds, coral,
moonstone, topazes, gold,
enamel, diamonds, platinum,
and mirror
10.4 x 6 x 2.2 cm
Cartier Collection, VC 41 A27

120. *Vanity case*
Cartier Paris, 1927
Ancient Egyptian calcite, gold,
enamel, coral, lapis lazuli,
emeralds, diamonds, platinum,
and mirror
9.9 x 5.2 x 2.1 cm
Sold to Ira Nelson Morris
Cartier Collection, VC 65 A27

121. *Inkwell* (pl. 81)
Cartier New York, ca. 1927
Porcelain, enamel, wood,
and gold
9.2 x 6.3 x 6.3 cm
Sold to Mona Travis Strader
(Mrs. Harrison Williams), later
Countess Mona Bismarck
Cartier Collection, DI 07 C27

122. *Visiting card with envelope*
(frontispiece, p. 1)
Cartier New York, ca. 1927
Gold and enamel
Inscription to Pierre and Elma
Cartier in handwriting of Louis
Cartier
5.1 x 8.4 cm
Sold to Louis Cartier
Cartier Collection, AG 76 C27

123. *Belt*
Cartier Paris, 1928
Diamonds, onyx, platinum, gold,
enamel, and satin
4.5 x 5 cm (buckle)
Cartier Collection, JA 14 A28

124. *Chimera bangle*
Cartier Paris, 1928
Coral, emeralds, sapphires, gold,
enamel, diamonds, and platinum
7.4 x 8.2 x 1.6 cm
Sold to Ganna Walska
(Mrs. Harold F. McCormick)
Cartier Collection, BT 109 A28

125. *Chinese-style vanity case*
Cartier Paris, 1928
Gold, enamel, onyx, emeralds,
rubies, sapphires, coral,
diamonds, platinum, and mirror
8.7 x 5.7 x 1.8 cm
Cartier Collection, VC 71 A28

126. *Cliquet pin*
Cartier New York, 1928
Diamonds and platinum
7 x 2 cm
Cartier Collection, CL 211 A28

127. *Cliquet pin*
Cartier New York, 1928
Diamonds and platinum
6.2 x 2.5 cm
Cartier Collection, CL 243 A28

128. *Cliquet pin*
Cartier Paris, 1928
Emeralds, rubies, sapphires,
pearls, diamonds, and platinum
7 x 3 cm
Sold to Helen Dinsmore
Huntington (Mrs. Vincent Astor)
California collection

129. *Desk clock*
Cartier New York, 1928
Gold, enamel, nephrite, coral,
clock movement, and glass
5.2 x 5.2 x 3 cm
Cartier Collection, CDS 89 A28

130. *Desk clock*
Cartier New York, 1928
Gold, onyx, enamel, clock
movement, and glass
5 x 5.4 x 2 cm
Sold to Harold F. McCormick
Cartier Collection, CDS 90 A28

131. Le Ciel *mystery clock* (pl. 163)
Cartier New York, 1928
Onyx, coral, jade, moonstones,
rock crystal, obsidian, gold,
enamel, mother-of-pearl,
diamonds, platinum, and clock
movement
21.9 x 7.6 x 1.6 cm
Siegelson, New York, F7134

132. *Pendant earrings*
Cartier New York, 1928
Jade, diamonds, platinum, and
enamel
5.9 x 1.9 cm (each of two earrings)
Cartier Collection, EG 11 A28

133. *Sautoir* (pl. 66)
Cartier Paris, 1928 (pendant) and
1929 (chain)
Diamonds and platinum
L. 79 cm
Cartier Collection, NE 14 A29

134. *Strap bracelet*
Cartier New York, 1928
Rubies, emeralds, sapphires,
diamonds, platinum, and enamel
3.4 x 19 cm
Cartier Collection, BT 12 A28

135. *Cigarette case and lighter*
Cartier Paris, ca. 1928
Gold, emeralds, diamonds,
moonstones, and enamel
10 x 5.7 x 1.7 cm (case), 3.6 x 3.6
x 1.4 cm (lighter)
Cartier Collection, CC 34 C28

136. *Chimera bracelet*
Cartier Paris, 1929
Diamonds, platinum, sapphires,
emeralds, and rock crystal
7.8 x 7.7 x 1.8 cm
Cartier Collection, BT 64 A29

137. *Cigarette box* (pl. 89)
Cartier Paris, 1929
Silver, gold, onyx, ebonite, and
enamel
22.2 x 32.5 x 10.5 cm
Engraved on cover: *Yacht Ara / to the
Commodore and Mrs. W. K. Vanderbilt /
"en souvenir" of the trip around the
world / November 1928–May 1929 /
Pierre*; at corners: *New York / Saigon /
Bombay / Monaco*
Provenance: William K. Vanderbilt, Jr.
Cartier Collection, TB 04 A29

138. *Cigarette case*
Cartier Paris, 1929
Gold, lapis lazuli, coral, ancient
Egyptian faience, mother-of-pearl,
diamonds, platinum, and enamel
8.3 x 5.2 x 2.9 cm
Sold to Ira Nelson Morris
Cartier Collection, CC 89 A29

139. *Desk watch* (pl. 88)
Cartier Paris, 1929
Gold, sapphires, enamel, watch
movement, and glass
4.3 x 3.6 cm
Sold to Douglas Fairbanks
Cartier Collection, WO 07 A29

140. *Evening bag* (pl. 86)
Cartier Paris, 1929
Gold, rubies, emeralds, diamonds,
platinum, enamel, and suede
Engraved inside frame:
*MRS. CONDE NAST 1040 PARK
AVENUE NEW YORK CITY*
15.5 x 16 x 5 cm
Sold to Leslie Foster
(Mrs. Condé Nast)
Cartier Collection, EB 05 A29

141. *Frame with portrait of Marjorie
Merriweather Post* (pl. 85)
Cartier Paris, 1929
Agate, gold, enamel, citrine,
diamonds, and watercolor on ivory
18.1 x 14.9 cm
Sold to Marjorie Merriweather Post
(Mrs. E. F. Hutton)
Hillwood Estate, Museum &
Gardens, bequest of Marjorie
Merriweather Post, 1973, 21.190

142. *Pair of clip brooches*
Cartier New York, 1929
Rubies, emeralds, diamonds,
platinum, white gold, and enamel
4.5 x 4.1 cm (each of two
brooches)
Cartier Collection, CL 31 A29

143. *Strap bracelet*
Cartier New York, 1929
Diamonds and platinum
2 x 18.1 cm
Cartier Collection, BT 97 A29

144. *Strap bracelet* (pl. 77)
Cartier Paris, 1929
Sapphires, emeralds, rubies,
diamonds, and platinum
4.1 x 18 cm
Sold to Linda Lee Thomas
(Mrs. Cole Porter)
Cartier Collection, BT 111 A29

145. *Tank cintrée wristwatch* (pl. 87)
Cartier London, 1929
Gold, sapphire cabochon, watch
movement, glass, and leather
Engraved on back of case: *Felix
from Fred '29*
4.6 x 2.3 cm (case)
Sold to Fred Astaire
Cartier Collection, WCL 113 A29

146. *Tortue wristwatch*
Cartier New York, 1929
Gold, watch movement, glass,
and leather
3.5 x 2.7 cm (case)
Sold to Edsel Ford
Cartier Collection, WCL 42 A29

147. *Watch brooch*
Cartier Paris, 1929
Jade, rubies, onyx, diamonds,
platinum, gold, enamel, glass,
and watch movement
Cartier Collection, WB 34 A29

148. *Baguette bracelet watch with
sliding cover*
Cartier Paris, 1930
Yellow gold, pink gold, watch
movement, and glass
3.5 x 1.8 cm (case)
Sold to Gloria Swanson,
Marquise de la Falaise
Cartier Collection, WWL 93 A30

149. *Belt* (pl. 82)
Cartier London, 1930
Jade, rubies, and gold
5 x 85.6 cm
Sold to Ganna Walska
(Mrs. Harold F. McCormick)
Cartier Collection, JA 26 A30

150. *Bracelets* (pl. 21)
Cartier Paris, 1930
Rock crystal, diamonds, and
platinum
7.5 x 2.9 x 1.2 cm and
7.9 x 2.7 x 1.6 cm
Sold to Gloria Swanson,
Marquise de la Falaise
Cartier Collection, BT 27 A30,
BT 28 A30

151. *Five-dial clock* (pl. 128)
Cartier New York, 1930
Onyx, silver, nephrite, and enamel
Engraved on plaque: *"L'HEURE
DE LA VICTOIRE DANS LE MONDE"
HOMMAGE À SON ARTISAN LE
PRESIDENT DES ETATS UNIS
FRANKLIN D. ROOSEVELT*
22 x 20 x 11 cm
Provenance: Franklin D. Roosevelt
Private collection

152. *Model of LeCoultre Caliber 101
watch movement*
Cartier New York, 1930
Gilded brass, watch movement,
and glass
Inscription on plaque to
Henry Ford
12.5 x 21 x 8 cm
Provenance: Henry Ford; Henry
Ford Museum
Cartier Collection, CDB 15 A30

153. *Sautoir*
Cartier London, 1930
Rubies, pearls, diamonds, and
platinum
L. 62.1 cm
Sold to Nancy Perkins (Mrs.
Ronald Tree), later Nancy
Lancaster
Cartier Collection, NE 27 A30

154. *Vanity case*
Cartier London, 1930
Gold, enamel, diamond, and
mirror
Engraved inside powder
compartment: *MARY PICKFORD*
4.5 x 6.5 x 1.3 cm
Sold to Mary Pickford
Cartier Collection, VC 75 A30

155. *Cocktail set* (pl. 96)
Cartier New York, ca. 1930
Silver and silver gilt
Monogram engraved on each item:
JCC
H. 20 cm (shaker), 20.5 cm (each of
two flasks), 12.5 cm (lemon squeezer),
4.5 cm (each of six tumblers)
Cartier Collection, SI 09 C30

156. *Evening bag*
Cartier, ca. 1930 (clasp)
Coral, emerald, diamonds,
platinum, and velvet
15.5 x 21 x 3.7 cm
Provenance: Jacqueline Bouvier
(Mrs. John F. Kennedy)
Cartier Collection, EB 31 C30

157. *Cigarette case* (pl. 94)
Cartier Paris, 1931
Platinum and diamond
7.3 x 7.8 x 1.1 cm
Back of lid and inside case
engraved with twenty signatures
Sold to Baron Adolf de Meyer
Cartier Collection, CC 50 A31

158. *Lipstick case*
Cartier New York, 1931
Gold, lacquer, and enamel
5.2 x 1.5 x 1.2 cm
Provenance: Vanderbilt family
Cartier Collection, AL 89 A31

159. *Striking mystery clock with
deity* (pl. 164)
Cartier Paris, 1931
White jade, nephrite, onyx, rock
crystal, gold, enamel, pearls,
turquoises, coral, diamonds,
platinum, and clock movement
35 x 28 x 14 cm
Sold to Paul Louis Weiller
Cartier Collection, CM 04 A31

160. *Case for gemstone*
Cartier New York, 1932
Gold
Engraved on cover: Russian
imperial coat of arms
3.7 x 4.1 x 1.4 cm
Cartier Collection, BS 01 A32

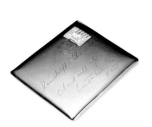

161. *Cigarette case* (pl. 95)
Cartier London, 1932
Gold and enamel
Inscription to Randolph
Churchill in handwriting of
Winston Churchill
8.8 x 10.5 x 1.1 cm
Sold to Winston Churchill
Cartier Collection, CC 39 A32

162. *Cigarette case* (pl. 92)
Cartier Paris, 1932
Gold, enamel, diamonds, and
platinum
9 x 8.5 x 1.7 cm
Provenance: Virginia Graham
Fair (formerly Mrs. William K.
Vanderbilt, Jr.)
Cartier Collection, CC 88 A32

163. *Cigarette case* (pl. 93)
Cartier London, 1932
Yellow gold, red gold, and
sapphire cabochons
Engraved inside cover: *Buck from
Sylvia and Douglas*
8 x 11.1 x .8 cm
Sold to Douglas Fairbanks
Cartier Collection, CC 99 A32

164. *Necklace* (pl. 120)
Cartier London, 1932
Diamonds, emerald, and
platinum
24 x 18.6 cm
Sold to Beatrice Mills,
Countess of Granard
Cartier Collection, NE 25 A32

165. *Cigarette case*
Cartier New York, 1933
Yellow gold, pink gold, enamel,
diamonds, rubies, and sapphires
7.5 x 13.8 x .8 cm
Provenance: Buddy DeSylva
Cartier Collection, CC 93 A33

166. *Ring*
Cartier New York, 1933
Coral, onyx, platinum, and
diamonds
2.3 x 2.7 x 2.1 cm
Sold to Marjorie Merriweather
Post (Mrs. E. F. Hutton)
Cartier Collection, RG 01 A33

167. *Ring* (pl. 138)
Cartier Paris, 1934
Jade, rubies, diamonds, and gold
2.9 x 2.9 x 2.1 cm
Sold to Barbara Hutton, Princess
Alexis Mdivani
Cartier Collection, RG 30 A34

168. *Ring*
Cartier New York, 1934
Platinum and emeralds
2.9 x 2.1 x 1.4 cm
Cartier Collection, RG 37 A34

169. *Tiara*
Cartier London, 1934
Diamonds and platinum
4 x 17 cm
Sold to Andrée Carron,
HH the Begum Aga Khan
Cartier Collection, HO 10 A34

170. *Bracelet*
Cartier New York, 1935
Pearls, diamonds, and platinum
2.5 x 16.5 cm
Provenance: Nanaline Holt Inman
(Mrs. James B. Duke);
Doris Duke
Siegelson, New York, F1 127

171. *Double clip brooch* (pl. 78)
Cartier Paris, 1935
Sapphires, rubies, emeralds,
diamonds, platinum, and osmior
4.5 x 9.8 cm
Sold to Linda Lee Thomas
(Mrs. Cole Porter)
Cartier Collection, CL 266 A35

172. *Pyramid clip brooch*
Cartier Paris, 1935
Diamonds and platinum
4.2 x 4.6 cm
Cartier Collection, CL 63 A35

173. *Vanity case* (pl. 119)
Cartier London, 1935
Gold, platinum, diamonds,
enamel, and mirror
Monogram on cover: BG
15.2 x 8.5 x 2.3 cm
Sold to Beatrice Mills, Countess
of Granard
Cartier Collection, VC 44 A35

174. *Bangle with clip brooches*
(pls. 117–118)
Cartier New York, 1936
Platinum, white gold, diamonds,
and lacquer
5.3 x 6 x 2.4 cm
Cartier Collection, BT 98 A36

175. *Cigarette case*
Cartier London, 1936
Gold and sapphires
8.9 x 6.8 x 1.7 cm
Cartier Collection, CC 66 A36

176. *Double clip brooch*
Cartier Paris, 1936
Diamonds and platinum
3.2 x 5.2 cm (each of two clips)
Cartier Collection, CL 192 A36

177. *"Hindu" necklace* (pl. 79)
Cartier Paris, 1936; altered 1963
Sapphires, emeralds, rubies,
diamonds, platinum, and white
gold
20 x 19 cm
Sold to Daisy Fellowes (Hon.
Mrs. Reginald Fellowes)
Cartier Collection, NE 28 A36

178. *Necklace*
Cartier New York, 1936 (clasp) and
1963 (pearls)
Pearls, diamonds, and platinum
L. 45.7 cm
Provenance: Marjorie Merriweather
Post (Mrs. Joseph E. Davies)
Hillwood Estate, Museum &
Gardens, bequest of Marjorie
Merriweather Post, 1973, 17.69

179. *Necklace and bracelet*
Cartier London, 1936
Peridots, diamonds, and platinum
22.6 x 15 cm (necklace),
3 x 17 cm (bracelet)
Cartier Collection, JS 06 A36

180. *Pyramid clip brooch*
Cartier New York, 1936
Diamonds, sapphire, and
platinum
3.9 x 3.6 cm
Cartier Collection, CL 204 A36

181. *Tiara* (pl. 113)
Cartier London, 1936
Turquoises, diamonds, and
platinum
4.8 x 15.5 cm
Sold to the Hon. Robert Henry
Brand
Cartier Collection, HO 06 A36

182. *Vanity case*
Cartier New York, 1936
Gold, diamonds, platinum, and
mirror
4.7 x 8.6 x 1.6 cm
Cartier Collection, VC 82 A36

183. *Bangle*
Cartier Paris, 1937
Diamonds and platinum
2.6 x 7 x 5.7 cm
Cartier Collection, BT 48 A37

184. *Clip brooch*
Cartier London, 1937
Gold
3 x 2 cm
Monogram: WE with coronet
Sold to HRH the Duke of Windsor
Cartier Collection, CL 86 A37

185. *Clip brooch* (pl. 115)
Cartier New York, 1937
Diamonds, emeralds, and
platinum
5.5 x 4.9 cm
Sold to Ellin Mackay
(Mrs. Irving Berlin)
Cartier Collection, CL 267 A37

186. *Necklace* (pl. 114)
Cartier New York, 1937
Sapphires, diamonds, and platinum
L. 43.2 cm
Provenance: Marjorie Merriweather
Post (Mrs. Joseph E. Davies)
Hillwood Estate, Museum &
Gardens, bequest of Marjorie
Merriweather Post, 1973, 17.68

187. *Orchid brooch* (pl. 107)
Cartier Paris, 1937
Amethysts, aquamarines, white
gold, and enamel
12.6 x 11.4 cm
Cartier Collection, CL 132 A37

188. *Pair of blackamoor clip brooches*
(pl. 110)
Cartier Paris, 1937
Gold, lacquer, turquoise, coral,
pearls, diamonds, and silver
3.5 x 1.7 cm (each of two brooches)
Sold to Prince Tikka Rajah of
Kapurthala
Cartier Collection, CL 65 A37

189. *Tiara*
Cartier London, 1937
Aquamarines, diamonds, and
platinum
5 x 17 cm
Cartier Collection, HO 12 A37

190. *Tiara*
Cartier London, 1937
Citrine, gold, diamonds, and
platinum
6 x 17 cm
Cartier Collection, HO 14 A37

191. *Bangle* (pls. 100–101)
Cartier Paris, 1938
Gold and lapis lazuli
DIAM. 8.1 cm
Cartier Collection, BT 124 A38

192. *Bracelet and ear clips*
Cartier Paris, 1938
Gold and sapphires
2.1 x 18 cm (bracelet), 3.6 x 1.8
cm (each of two ear clips)
Cartier Collection, JS 05 A38

193. *Bracelet watch*
Cartier Paris, 1938
Gold, citrines, watch movement,
and glass
DIAM. 5.7 cm
Cartier Collection, WWL 71 A38

194. *Rose clip brooch*
Cartier Paris, 1938
Gold, enamel, diamonds, silver,
and platinum
4.5 x 2.6 cm
Cartier Collection, CL 25 A38

195. *Rose clip brooch*
Cartier Paris, 1938
Gold, coral, diamonds, platinum,
and enamel
4 x 2.5 cm
Cartier Collection, CL 184 A38

196. *Rose clip brooch* (pl. 116)
Cartier London, 1938
Diamonds and platinum
7.3 x 4.3 cm
Provenance: HRH Princess
Margaret, Countess of Snowdon
Cartier Collection, CL 296 A38

197. *Sioux clip brooch* (pl. 108)
Cartier Paris, 1938
Gold, lacquer, diamonds,
turquoise cabochons, and silver
3.1 x 3 cm
Cartier Collection, CL 275 A38

198. *Squaw clip brooch* (pl. 109)
Cartier Paris, 1938
Gold, lacquer, diamonds, and
silver
3.3 x 3 cm
Cartier Collection, CL 280 A38

199. *Bangle with flower clip brooch*
Cartier Paris, 1939
Diamonds, platinum, and white
gold
DIAM. 5 cm (bracelet), 6 x 6 cm
(brooch)
Sold to a member of the
Romanian royal family
Cartier Collection, BT 116 A39

200. *Bracelet watch*
Cartier New York, 1939
Gold, sapphires, watch
movement, and glass
L. 19 cm
Cartier Collection, WWL 94 A39

201. *Handcuff bracelet* (pl. 102)
Cartier Paris, 1939
Gold, amethysts, and citrines
DIAM. 7.5 cm
Cartier Collection, BT 105 A39

202. *Snow White and the Seven
Dwarfs charm bracelet*
Cartier New York, 1939
Gold and enamel
L. 18 cm
Cartier Collection, BT 122 A39

203. *Bracelet watch with
sliding case*
Cartier New York, 1940
Pink gold, green gold, platinum,
diamonds, watch movement,
and glass
3 x 18.6 cm
Cartier Collection, WWL 92 A40

204. *Flamingo clip brooch* (pl. 125)
Cartier Paris, 1940
Diamonds, emeralds, rubies,
sapphires, citrine, and platinum
9.8 x 6.4 cm
Sold to HRH the Duke of Windsor
Private collection

205. *Hand mirror*
Cartier New York, 1940
Gold, nephrite, jade, cornaline,
and coral cabochons
25.6 x 10.4 x 1.5 cm
Sold to Jessie May Woolworth
(Mrs. James P. Donahue)
Cartier Collection, AL 114 A40

206. *Necklace*
Cartier Paris, 1940; altered 1972
Coral, pearls, onyx, emeralds,
diamonds, platinum, and enamel
L. APPROX. 40 cm
Provenance: María Félix
California collection

207. *Brooch*
Cartier Paris, 1942
Gold, emeralds, diamonds, and
platinum
5 x 4 cm
Cartier Collection, CL 304 A42

208. *Shell brooch*
Cartier New York, 1942
Lion's paw shell, sapphires,
turquoise, and gold
7.4 x 7.7 cm
Cartier Collection, CL 295 A42

209. *Gremlin charm bracelet*
Cartier London, 1942–1943
Gold and enamel
L. 17 cm
Cartier Collection, BT 73 C43

210. *Flower clip brooch*
Cartier London, 1943
Topaz, citrines, gold, diamonds,
and platinum
11 x 5 cm
Provenance: Lydia Pavlovna
Kondoyarova, Lady Deterding
Cartier Collection, CL 233 A43

211. *Laurel clip brooch*
Cartier Paris, 1943
Gold, sapphires, diamonds, and
platinum
9 x 4.5 cm
Cartier Collection, CL 180 A43

212. *Commemorative plaque* (pl. 129)
Cartier New York, ca. 1943
Silver
Inscription: *TO ALAN MOWBRAY*
WITH THE AFFECTIONATE REGARDS
OF THE LONG STEMMED AMERICAN
BEAUTIES
18.4 x 10.7 cm
Provenance: Alan Mowbray
Collection of Neil Lane, Los
Angeles

213. *Bird clip brooch*
Cartier Paris, 1944
Gold, emeralds, sapphires, rubies,
diamonds, and platinum
9 x 7.1 cm
Cartier Collection, CL 191 A44

214. *Brooch*
Cartier Paris, 1944
Gold, lapis lazuli, coral, sapphire
cabochon, diamonds, and platinum
Inscription: *1946 WILL BE BETTER*
DIAM. 3.1 cm
Cartier Collection, CL 298 A44

215. *Bird clip brooch*
Cartier Paris, 1944–1947
Gold, ruby, emerald, diamonds,
and platinum
5.6 x 3 cm
Cartier Collection, CL 126 A47

216. *Bracelet*
Cartier Paris, 1945
Yellow gold and red gold
2.6 x 19 cm
Cartier Collection, BT 63 A45

217. *Bracelet* (pl. 103)
Cartier New York, ca. 1945
Pink gold, sapphires, diamonds,
and platinum
DIAM. 5 cm
Cartier Collection, BT 123 C45

218. *Patriotic clip brooch*
Cartier New York, ca. 1945
Gilt metal and enamel
Inscription: *FRIENDS OF SOLDIERS*
AND SAILORS NEW YORK STATE
3.8 x 4.5 x 2.4 cm
Collection of Neil Lane,
Los Angeles

219. *Powder case* (pl. 105)
Cartier New York, 1946
Gold, rubies, and mirror
Inscription: *CL / V+L / 1952*
6.6 x 7.7 x 1.4 cm
Sold to Vivien Leigh
Cartier Collection, PB 30 A46

220. *Bib necklace* (pl. 122)
Cartier Paris, 1947
Gold, amethysts, turquoises,
diamonds, and platinum
20 x 19.5 cm
Sold to HRH the Duke of Windsor
Cartier Collection, NE 09 A47

221. *Coffee bean watch brooch*
Cartier New York, 1947
Gold, diamonds, platinum, watch
movement, and glass
DIAM. 5.4 cm
Cartier Collection, WB 38 A47

222. Oiseau libéré *brooch* (pl. 112)
Cartier Paris, 1947
Gold, coral, lapis lazuli,
diamonds, platinum, and sapphire
3.6 x 2.3 cm
Cartier Collection, CL 299 A47

223. *Ring*
Cartier Paris, 1947
Gold, coral, emeralds, diamonds,
and platinum
3.8 x 3 x 3 cm
Sold to Wallis Warfield, Duchess
of Windsor
Cartier Collection, RG 33 A47

224. *Buckle bracelet and
ear clips* (pl. 106)
Cartier New York, 1948
Gold, sapphires, diamonds, and
platinum
3.1 x 20 cm (bracelet), 2.2 x 1.5
cm (each of two ear clips)
Cartier Collection, JS 07 A48

225. *Ring*
Cartier Paris, 1948
Gold and sapphires
2.7 x 3.1 x 1.8 cm
Provenance: Daisy Fellowes
(Hon. Mrs. Reginald Fellowes)
Cartier Collection, RG 40 A48

226. *Flower brooch*
Cartier New York, ca. 1948
Pink gold, rubies, diamonds, and
platinum
4.9 x 4.8 cm
Cartier Collection, CL 297 C48

227. *Panther clip brooch* (pl. 123)
Cartier Paris, 1949
Sapphires, diamonds, yellow
diamonds, platinum, and white
gold
6 x 3.7 cm
Sold to HRH the Duke of Windsor
Cartier Collection, CL 53 A49

228. *Clip brooch*
Cartier New York, 1950
Diamonds and platinum
19.7 x 5.7 cm
Sold to Marjorie Merriweather
Post (Mrs. Joseph E. Davies)
Hillwood Estate, Museum &
Gardens, bequest of Marjorie
Merriweather Post, 1973, 17.82

229. *Necklace* (pl. 121)
Cartier New York, 1950
Amethysts, turquoises, diamonds,
gold, and platinum
L. 45.7 cm
Sold to Marjorie Merriweather
Post (Mrs. Joseph E. Davies)
Hillwood Estate, Museum &
Gardens, bequest of Marjorie
Merriweather Post, 1973, 17.67.1

230. *Cowboy duck brooch* (pl. 111)
Cartier New York, ca. 1950
Gold, white chalcedony, coral,
and sapphire
5 x 1.9 cm
Cartier Collection, CL 302 C50

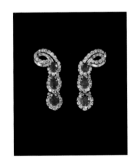

231. *Bracelet* (pl. 142)
Cartier Paris, 1951
Rubies, diamonds, and platinum
2.2 x 15.6 cm
Sold to Mike Todd in 1957
Collection of Dame Elizabeth
Taylor

232. *Earrings* (pl. 141)
Cartier Paris, 1951
Rubies, diamonds, and platinum
5.7 x 2.5 cm (each of two earrings)
Sold to Mike Todd in 1957
Collection of Dame Elizabeth
Taylor

233. *Necklace* (pl. 143)
Cartier Paris, 1951
Rubies, diamonds, and platinum
L. 17.2 cm
Sold to Mike Todd in 1957
Collection of Dame Elizabeth
Taylor

234. *Panther bracelet* (pl. 124)
Cartier Paris, 1952
Diamonds, onyx, emeralds, and
platinum
2.5 x 19.1 cm
Sold to Wallis Warfield, Duchess
of Windsor
Private collection

235. *Strap bracelet*
Cartier Paris, 1952
Yellow gold and pink gold
2 x 17.5 cm
Provenance: Barbara Hutton
Cartier Collection, BT 60 A52

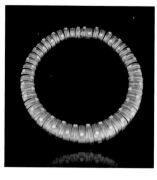

236. *Bangle*
Cartier Paris, 1953
Yellow gold, white gold,
turquoises, and diamonds
6.5 x 7.1 cm
Sold to a member of the
Rothschild family
Cartier Collection, BT 104 A53

237. *Duck head clip brooch*
Cartier Paris, 1953
Blister pearl, coral, sapphire,
emeralds, gold, diamond, and
platinum
4.2 x 4.8 cm
Sold to Wallis Warfield,
Duchess of Windsor
Cartier Collection, CL 127 A53

238. *Necklace*
Cartier Paris, 1953
Amethysts, gold, and turquoises
L. 34.6 cm
Sold to Daisy Fellowes (Hon.
Mrs. Reginald Fellowes)
Cartier Collection, NE 37 A53

239. *Necklace* (pl. 145)
Cartier Paris, 1953
Diamonds and platinum
L. 38 cm
Provenance: Grace Kelly,
Princess of Monaco
Palais Princier de Monaco,
PO11495

240. *Necklace* (pl. 104)
Cartier Paris, 1953
Gold, diamonds, and platinum
L. 38.1 cm
Sold to Daisy Fellowes
(Hon. Mrs. Reginald Fellowes)
Private collection

241. *Wristwatch*
Cartier Paris, 1953
Gold, watch movement, glass,
and leather
DIAM. 2.5 cm (case)
Sold to Barbara Hutton, Baroness
von Cramm
Cartier Collection, WCL 114 A53

242. *Tiger lorgnette* (pl. 126)
Cartier Paris, 1954
Gold, glass, enamel, and emeralds
8.5 x 2.2 cm (closed)
Provenance: Wallis Warfield,
Duchess of Windsor
Cartier Collection, OI 08 A54

243. *Bib necklace* (pl. 134)
Cartier Paris, 1955
Gold, diamonds, and turquoises
19.3 x 16.5 cm
Cartier Collection, NE 31 A55

244. *Bracelet*
Cartier Paris, 1955
Platinum and diamonds
6 x 7 x 1.5 cm
Provenance: Grace Kelly, Princess
of Monaco
Palais Princier de Monaco,
PO11406

245. *Pug clip brooch* (pl. 127)
Cartier Paris, 1955
Enamel, gold, and citrines
3.3 x 2.4 cm
Sold to HRH the Duke of Windsor
in 1956
Cartier Collection, CL 251 A55

246. *Set of clip brooches* (pl. 146)
Cartier Paris, 1955
Diamonds, rubies, platinum,
and gold
4.6 x 5.5 cm (each of three brooches)
Provenance: Grace Kelly,
Princess of Monaco
Palais Princier de Monaco, PO11322

247. *Bird brooch* (pl. 148)
Cartier Paris, ca. 1955
Gold, platinum, and diamonds
3.5 x 3.5 cm
Provenance: Grace Kelly,
Princess of Monaco
Palais Princier de Monaco,
PO11249

248. *Miniature prism clock*
Cartier Paris, ca. 1955
Gold, platinum, diamonds, rock
crystal, and clock movement
8 x 4.8 x 4.8 cm
Provenance: Grace Kelly,
Princess of Monaco
Palais Princier de Monaco, PO05989

249. *Bird brooch* (pl. 149)
Cartier London, 1956
Gold, emerald, pearls, and coral
3 x 2.5 cm
Provenance: Grace Kelly,
Princess of Monaco
Palais Princier de Monaco,
PO11253

250. *Bracelet*
Cartier Paris, 1956
Sapphires, gold, and platinum
L. 19 cm
Sold to a member of the
Rothschild family
Cartier Collection, BT 101 A56

251. *Engagement ring* (pl. 144)
Cartier Paris, 1956
Diamonds and platinum
2.3 x 1.6 x 1.1 cm
Provenance: Grace Kelly,
Princess of Monaco
Palais Princier de Monaco,
PO11276

252. *Mystery clock with single axle*
Cartier Paris, 1956
Gold, smoky quartz, diamonds,
platinum, silver gilt, and clock
movement
21 x 17 x 8.5 cm
Cartier Collection, CM 15 A56

253. *Evening bag*
Cartier New York, 1957
Gold, coral, emeralds, sapphires,
diamonds, platinum, and velvet
17 x 18 x 1.2 cm
Provenance: María Félix
Cartier Collection, EB 25 A57

254. *Hen brooch*
Cartier Paris, 1957
Gold, platinum, diamonds,
emerald, mother-of pearl, pearls,
and coral
4.5 x 3.1 cm
Provenance: Grace Kelly,
Princess of Monaco
Palais Princier de Monaco,
PO11171

255. *Tiger clip brooch* (pl. 139)
Cartier Paris, 1957
Gold, onyx, diamonds, and
emeralds
7 x 4.5 cm
Sold to Barbara Hutton,
Baroness von Cramm
Cartier Collection, CL 140 A57

256. *Blue rose clip brooch* (pl. 135)
Cartier Paris, 1959
Sapphires, diamonds, platinum,
and white gold
4.5 x 4 cm
Cartier Collection, CL 55 A59

257. *Necklace*
Cartier New York, 1959
Diamonds and platinum
DIAM. 14.3 cm
Collection of Neil Lane,
Los Angeles

258. *Tank wristwatch*
Cartier Paris, 1959
Yellow gold, pink gold, sapphire,
watch movement, and glass
3 x 2.3 cm (case)
Sold to Elizabeth Taylor
Cartier Collection, WCL 37 A59

259. *Bracelet* (pl. 136)
Cartier New York, ca. 1960
Sapphires, diamonds, and
platinum
2.3 x 17.2 cm
Collection of Diane B. Wilsey

260. *Poodle brooch* (pl. 147)
Cartier London, ca. 1960
Gold, platinum, ruby, pearls,
and onyx
4 x 1.5 cm
Provenance: Grace Kelly,
Princess of Monaco
Palais Princier de Monaco,
PO11250

261. *Chimera bangle*
Cartier Paris, 1961
Coral, diamonds, platinum,
and emeralds
5.9 x 7.4 cm
Provenance: Daisy Fellowes
(Hon. Mrs. Reginald Fellowes)
Cartier Collection, BT 52 A61

262. *Evening bag*
Cartier Paris, 1961
Gold, enamel, diamonds,
emeralds, and satin
Monogram: *N* with coronet
20 x 27 x 5.5 cm
Provenance: Barbara Hutton;
Princess Nina Mdivani
Cartier Collection, EB 15 A61

263. *Extra-thin wristwatch*
Cartier Paris, 1961
Gold, watch movement, glass,
and leather
DIAM. 3.1 cm (case)
Sold to Stewart Granger
Cartier Collection, WWG 14 A61

264. *Tiger ear clips* (pl. 140)
Cartier Paris, 1961
Gold, onyx, diamonds, and
emeralds
5.1 x 3 cm (each of two ear clips)
Sold to Barbara Hutton
Cartier Collection, EG 07 A61

265. *Oblique wristwatch*
Cartier London, 1963
Yellow gold, pink gold, sapphire,
watch movement, glass, and
leather
3.4 x 2.3 cm (case)
Sold to Stewart Granger
Cartier Collection, WCL 52 A63

266. *Pendant earrings*
Cartier Paris, 1963
Emeralds, diamonds, platinum, white gold, yellow gold, and enamel
5.2 x 1.9 cm (each of two earrings)
Sold to Daisy Fellowes (Hon. Mrs. Reginald Fellowes) as a hatpin in 1939 and altered in 1945 as a necklace clasp; remade as earrings for the Comtesse de Castéja
Cartier Collection, EG 28 A63

267. *Brush set* (pl. 152)
Cartier London, 1966
Gold, lapis lazuli, and bristles
Monogram on each brush: SG
17.8 x 4.4 cm (one brush), 13.9 x 8.6 cm (each of two brushes)
Provenance: Stewart Granger
Cartier Collection, AG 81 A66

268. *Universal time clock*
Cartier Paris, 1966
Gold, coral, silver, diamonds, clock movement, and glass
9 x 8.2 cm
Sold to Barbara Hutton, Princess Doan Vinh na Champassak
Cartier Collection, CDS 64 A66

269. *Flower ear clips*
Cartier Paris, 1967
Gold, diamonds, rubies, emeralds, sapphires, and platinum
2.9 x 2.7 cm (flowers open)
Cartier Collection, EG 15 A67

270. *Leaf-shaped ear clips* (pl. 132)
Cartier Paris, 1967; altered 1976
Emeralds and gold
5 x 4 cm
Provenance: María Félix; Doris Duke
California collection

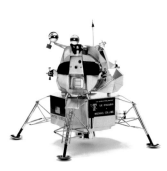

271. *Mystery clock with single axle*
Cartier Paris, 1967
Gold, lapis lazuli, diamonds, platinum, rock crystal, and clock movement
15.5 x 8.1 x 4.7 cm
Provenance: Barbara Hutton, Princess Doan Vinh na Champassak
Cartier Collection, CM 17 A67

272. *Snake necklace* (pl. 151)
Cartier Paris, 1968
Diamonds, platinum, white gold, yellow gold, emeralds, and enamel
L. 57 cm
Sold to María Félix
Cartier Collection, NE 10 A68

273. *Dolphin bangle* (pl. 137)
Cartier Paris, 1969
Gold, diamonds, and emeralds
9 x 8.1 x 5.7 cm
Cartier Collection, BT 115 A69

274. *Replica of Apollo 11 lunar module* (pl. 153)
Cartier Paris, 1969
Yellow gold, white gold, lacquer, and enamel
25 x 15 x 10 cm
Provenance: Michael Collins
Cartier Collection, OV 11 A69

275. *Crocodile necklace* (pl. 150)
Cartier Paris, 1975
Gold, diamonds, emeralds, and rubies
L. 30 cm and 27.3 cm (each of two segments)
Sold to María Félix
Cartier Collection, NE 43 A75

276. *Paperweight*
Cartier New York, 1977
Platinum, gold, diamonds, and ebony
8.6 x 8.7 x 8.7 cm
Cartier Collection, DI 18 A77

277. *Flamingo clip brooch*
Cartier Paris, 1987
Diamonds, rubies, sapphires, emeralds, citrine, and platinum
10 x 6 cm
California collection

278. *Parrot clip brooch*
Cartier Paris, 1992
Diamonds, rubies, sapphires, emeralds, onyx, and gold
5.1 x 7.6 cm
Private collection

279. *Orchid necklace* (pl. 31)
Cartier Paris, 2007
Beryl, pink sapphires, diamonds, and platinum
L. 35.6 cm, H. 3.8 cm (pendant)
Private collection